CU00823482

INTRODUCTION

My mother said I should write a book about being a vet, so I did! There are many amusing tales from my life as a vet, as well as some heart warming stories, unbelievable situations and very sad moments. Given so many people ask what I like best about my job, I decided to call the book Stuff Vets Like. This started off as a blog but I realised that each blog post made a neat little chapter so thought I'd convert it into a book. So welcome to Stuff Vets Like, an attempt at some amusing tales from the life of a veterinary surgeon; a place to read about the things that vets like to see in their pet patients, human clients and places they work. The majority of the time these are based on my own or my colleagues 'experiences. I worked at a reasonably large, very busy independent practice for over six years. I loved that job and hope to return in the future but right now, I am working as a locum (like a vet contractor who covers holiday, maternity leave or fills a gap whilst practices are trying to recruit a permanent vet). This is to gain freedom and a higher income in order to travel the world before settling down in a couple of years. I do love my job as a vet and feel lucky to be part of such a wonderful profession but it can be very tough so some chapters do get emotional (and sometimes I go off on a rant). I hope you enjoy reading it, that you find it informative or it at least gives you a giggle in places.

STUFF VETS LIKE:

ANIMALS

Yes, seems like an obvious place to start but people do seem to forget this at times. We enter into this profession because all of us love animals. What is the first question most people ask a vet? Yep, you guessed right - what is your favourite animal? My favourite is an elephant, but dogs are in the top three and cats definitely battle it out for a place in the top five. As much as I wish someone would bring an elephant into the practice, I have to settle for dogs and cats most of the time. I could spend some time with farm animals and horses too if I went to a practice that treated all animals but I decided I didn't want to spend half of my life smelling like cow poo or with my arm up a cow's bottom just to keep warm. Plus horsey people scare me. Over the course of a day, I probably spend about twenty minutes just stroking and playing with the animals that come to see me whilst I chat to the owners. If there is a particularly cute pet in the kennels for an operation or as an inpatient, word soon gets around the practice and we will often take a few minutes out of the day to go for a cuddle. So I do get paid to cuddle animals - for a short period of time!

My brother and I are both vets and we have wanted to enter into the profession as long as either of us can remember. We were lucky enough to grow up in the countryside, surrounded by farm animals in the fields around, wild animals in the garden and woodlands, and our own dogs throughout our childhood. We have always loved nature and especially the animals that were around us. This love of animals is the reason that every vet and vet nurse that I know of wanted to become what they are today. Animals have the ability to tune into your emotions as much as, and sometimes more than, people can. Who do you prefer, animals or people? Yes, good answer (I'm assuming you said animals because that's obviously the right answer). If somebody is an animal lover, animals can tell and if for some crazy reason they don't love animals, most of them instinctively know to steer clear. They can be very astute and know to be careful around small children. Dogs can be super boisterous and jumping all over you as a fully grown adult, but be gentle and not jump at toddlers. My cat, Lily, is very tolerant of my neighbours' children as they are young and don't quite understand to stroke her gently, but she never turns to scratch them. They can feel a range of emotions from joy and excitement to fear, sadness and even grief. I have lost count of the number of animals who pine for lost companions, both animal and human alike.

There are the times that they can make us laugh even in the toughest times. There is a reason most popular memes and videos on streaming services are just animals doing silly things. Yes, most of the time we are laughing at them because they are idiots but it's still entertaining. What's not to love about a dog playing in a paddling pool or barking at their reflection? Or a cat being terrified by the presence of a cucumber? Dogs will lick away your tears and jump up on your sofa beside you, or sometimes get as much of their body on top of you as they possibly can, knowing that you need a cuddle.

They are fantastic company to any person who lives on their own or feels isolated for any reason. My cat would always come to the door whenever I returned home from work, back when I was single (yes, I owned a cat way before I had a boyfriend, what are you implying?) To have another living being in the house makes you feel much less alone, giving you someone to talk to even though they can't answer you back - most of the time! Lily and I used to have conversations back and forth for about ten seconds every day when I'd come in, with her meowing her 'hello 'and me returning that meow back and forth, until I would giggle at my own insanity and stop. I'm not dispelling the weird, spinster vibes am I?

One of my clients would tell me of a game she would play with her cat; she would put various small objects on the arms of the sofa and the cat would bat them off in turn, clearly enjoying the way she was interacting with her owner (and creating havoc in the process, as only cats think is a good thing to do). This same cat would sit outside the shower every time her owner was in there, and would lick the water from her legs when she got out; we all know cats prefer not to drink out of a bowl and will find literally anything else to provide their water, but this is something I hadn't heard before! This client was happily married by the way, though he did travel a lot. It wasn't like I was getting ideas and inspiration about how to continue along the crazy, cat lady route. I really do just find this adorable and shows the bond humans and animals can have. Most people think cats are evil and always plotting your death but I have only found this to be true about half of the time, the rest of them are pretty cute.

I know that animals have been a blessing to a lot of elderly and vulnerable people, giving a constant source of love and a reason to get out and go for a walk. Even my friend's rabbit and guinea pigs have given her a lot of laughs over the years. Pepper is one sassy bunny and will not let you stroke her except from the tip of her nose to the base of her ears. She may be a little diva, but you can't help but laugh when she goes running round in circles waiting for her treat, or feel a glow within when she does the cutest little bunny yawn. Then there are those people that tell me their rats, hamsters, snakes or lizards also give them such joy; no matter how small, pets still take up a large space in your heart. One of my friends once remarked that he would happily sit and watch some ducks for hours because he found them so fascinating and cute. I think he felt the same way about squirrels. He is a bit odd though.

So that is why all vets and vet nurses do what we do - because we care about your animals and want to make them better. There are times when the pets seem reasonably pleased to see me too which is always a joyous moment. I would say about a fifth of dogs and cats aren't exactly a vet's greatest fan (meaning they want to eat us and kill our family members whilst they sleep). There are a large percentage that are rather indifferent towards us, some of whom I may force a cuddle out of. Then there are about a quarter of them that are so unbelievably happy to see you and these are the ones that become our favourites. There have been many times that I have turned to clients and told them that pets like theirs are the reason I became a vet. These are the dogs that wag their tails and run around the consult room, trying to jump on your lap and give you licks. I have lost count of the times I have actually had a dog snog me - tongue in mouth whilst trying to speak to the owner. Given its not made me ill yet, it is something I don't mind too much, though when I'm later told that they eat their own poo, I swiftly stand up from the floor or take a step away from the consult table. Some large breed dogs are so soppy that they will just stand there and lean into you, slowly toppling you over, or allowing you to put your arms round their necks and giving them a big hug. Cats can be very affectionate towards us too; roaming around the consult room and weaving in and out of our legs, or rubbing their heads against our hands as we are trying to examine them.

During the coronavirus pandemic, we had been taking the pets away from the owners who were waiting out in the carpark, and examining them in the consult rooms with nurses holding them. There were a couple of occasions when I would turn around from writing some notes on the computer to see one or two nurses with dog hair all over them, sitting on the floor with a dog in each of their laps, just sitting and being stroked, happy as anything. There was another time I was alone in the room with a cat, again typing up the notes on the computer and it just leapt from the table onto my lap and contently purred until I was finished and put it back in its basket to take outside.

In more normal circumstances, there are a few dogs that stick firmly in my mind as the ones who bring me so much happiness when I see them. The first two are a golden retriever and a Labrador, who will normally be waiting patiently with the owner in the waiting room. As soon as I come into the room to call them in, they will virtually tug the owner's arms out of their sockets and jump up onto me, one on each hip with their paws around my waist. Who doesn't love a hug from a dog? Maybe if you're very short and it is a Great Dane. Or if it is a chihuahua and it just looks like it is humping your leg instead. Anyway, this is often to the amusement of everyone else in the waiting room until the dogs finally realise that I can't walk with them attached to me and we make our way into the consult.

The second dog is a Labrador who belongs to the owner's young, blind son as his 'Buddy dog'. She is a dog that is so very well behaved when she has her Guide Dogs jacket on, knowing that she must be sensible and calm when this is on. When you then take this off, she instantly becomes more playful and silly like most Labradors are! That a dog can be so incredibly clever and sensitive makes me smile every time. Though there are some Guide Dogs that are so clever that they have learnt to play tricks on their owner. One visually impaired owner once told me that he lets his dog run around the park and play with other dogs if he knows it is a safe area. She will then always come back to him when she is called but because she was clearly a psychopath in a former life, she stays just out of reach. Cue the blind man trying to clip her harness back on whilst not wandering in the direction of the nearest road or river. She repeats this several times before she allows herself to become a Guide Dog once more. Is anyone watching this and just thinking she's the world's worst Guide Dog? Probably.

Even when not at work, I still love to spend time with animals. If I am out for a walk and there is a friendly dog coming towards us, I will always go out of my way to go and give it a cuddle. This is much to the annoyance of anyone I am with at the time, often being slightly embarrassing and talking in that high pitched voice that we all do and most people pretend they don't. Some of the time I will even say hello to the owners, but I find the dogs more rewarding. In those situations where one can safely stroke a cat when out and about, I will likely crouch down and make noises to try to coax that cat towards me so I can give it a chin rub. If I go to any new area of the country or world on holiday, one of the first things you can see me doing is looking up where I can see any animals. Good job my boyfriend and most of my friends like animals too or I'd be a terrible holiday companion. Maybe I am anyway. I often get comments from family and friends laughing and asking how I never get bored of animals given I work with them most days. Well, the answer is obviously simple; animals will never stop bringing me joy. Pets tend to spend their lives giving joy to the owners and any animal lover that they come across. Why would I not want to spend my day interacting with them?

NICE CLIENTS

As much as we are here to help animals, the large majority of the time we are also helping the owner of that animal. Let me tell you, some of the time we are treating the owner *more* than we are the pet. Group therapy anyone? After we have given some medication and advice that will help improve the pet's health and return it to a happier state, the owner will also feel better. Some owners will then return to you personally the next time that pet needs something routine, or if they become ill again and need further treatment. These clients are the ones that will then become our favourites (though sometimes not, if they are one of the more strange people in life. Or the ones that smell a bit funny). We will start to have conversations about the animal's life outside of the vets, then onto our personal lives. After over seven years treating the same animals, I now have some clients that I would consider my friends rather than just clients. I know my colleagues are the same, from the vets to the nurses and the receptionists too. These are the people that you are happy to see on your consult list, knowing you'll have a few minutes of chatting as well as a cuddle of the animal.

One of my clients, Mrs Meridale, has owned multiple pugs over the last few years as well as a couple of cats, meaning that she has had many trips to the vets. Whenever she comes in, we will spend the first half of the consult talking about the pet and sorting any issues out but as I am drawing up medication or sending the notes through to reception, we will be having a chat about her daughter's latest drama or the neighbours being loud. I'm sure my advice was about as useful as painting your dog's toenails (something I've seen) but hopefully she felt better for having a rant. We also like to compare the latest gin to be found on the shelves, something that has swayed my consumer decisions many times. Whenever the dogs need their nails clipping, they are booked in with the same nurse every time, partly because she has the technique for these particular dogs down to a tee, but also because the client wants to be kept abreast of the latest news in the nurse's love life or holiday adventures. By the way, the technique to clip the nails of this particular dog is to let her lick peanut butter off a lollipop stick to distract her. If you don't, she gets very annoyed, turns a beautiful shade of blue and passes out. You've got to love pugs, right?

The owner of the two dogs that leap on me in the waiting room, Miss Barnaby, is also one of my favourite people to see. She has such amusing tales from her dating life, always telling me the latest message she's received from a particularly creepy guy on an app (of which there are a lot - boys, stop sending photos of your genitals) or the gorgeous man she went on a date with the previous week. We once had to make her dogs vomit out of hours because she'd come home to find her diet pill packets strewn all over the floor - something that could make them seriously ill if they'd eaten a lot of them. That's one way of dieting that she will never be trying again!

There aren't many jobs where you get to hear about such a wide variety of topics and walks of life. One lady who works for a cat charity comes to see me regularly with the next stray cat that she's found. There are a couple of cats that she has looked after that she ends up keeping, one of whom is named after me. One day, said cat got stuck up a tree and had to be rescued. I'm not sure how I feel about having this particular animal as my namesake.

Then there is Goldie's owner who brings him in for regular steroid injections for his feline asthma. She will often come in with her best friend and we will all have a giggle at the latest political or social situation and put the world to rights. When two cute, fluffy little cavachons come in with their owner, we discuss our trips to Cornwall and let each other know the places to go. Then there's the owner of a chocolate Labrador with particularly disastrous front wrists and paws who has some interesting tales from his job as a fireman. There are some of the more elderly clients who always give me inspiration for my later years - one lady lost her husband years ago and is still going on exotic holidays around the world, always planning the next trip as soon as she's back from this one. Another lady will joke and make comments about her youth and the way she acted and rebelled. There was the elderly gentleman who would always tell me a crude joke whenever he brought his dog in to see me.

One couple in their mid seventies had a collie who was on special low fat food for her pancreatitis that we would send to one of our branch practices for them to collect every few weeks. They'd always come in on a Friday afternoon when I was there and if I didn't have any clients waiting at the time, the receptionist and I would hear the latest about the grandchildren and the next trip to Madeira, a holiday I have been invited on multiple times! Mrs would always be complaining about how Mr was annoying her that week and telling us about her very good looking doctor, whilst Mr was moaning about how Mrs spent all the money on frivolous things.

Even if they are not your favourite, regular clients it is still lovely to have clients that are nice people. They can still be great to talk to or brighten up your day in some way. Some of them are very eccentric in their choice of clothing or hair colour and will be the same with their pets, having multiple outfits to match each other. A little Yorkie that I have been seeing recently has now come in dressed as a minion, in a biker jacket, in a kimono and in a waterproof onesie. Slightly unnecessary of course but the dog is actually not a spoilt brat and it does her no harm to wear these outfits! (The owner isn't matching in this circumstance, just before you have pictures of a large minion walking a tiny minion on a lead).

Some clients are exceedingly lovely but not the brightest of sparks, meaning that your consult is that little bit more tough. Take one conversation I had with an owner about 5 years ago now:

Me: Very sorry, we don't have your regular 20mg tablets in stock so instead of giving half a 20mg tablet each day, you can give two 5mg tablets. It will be the same price as usual. It says the dose on the label so it is written down.

Client: But 5mg isn't enough, she's normally on 20mg tablets.

Me: You normally give half a 20mg tablet which makes 10mg. The new tablets are 5mg tablets but if you give two of them then that adds up to 10mg.

Client: But I normally have 20mg tablets.

Me: Yes, which is 10mg when you give half. Two 5's make 10, half of 20 is 10. Do you think that's ok?

Client: Yes, I think I get it now.

Me: Ok, fantastic. Here are your 5mg tablets. Can I just check, how many will you give each day?

Client: One. (Looks delighted with herself).

These clients definitely still fall under the nice client category but they are not the ones you want on your list as you know that you will run behind quite easily due to the explaining you are going to need to do!

There are some clients that just tell you fantastic stories about their animals that cause such entertainment. Rose is a rather regal cat who is a posh pedigree breed but doesn't know it as she is happy to interact with the local wildlife in an incredible way. The owners have witnessed her going to the bottom of the garden to play with a fox and her cubs. She goes down there every night as it is getting dark and they see them come out to play with each other. She even teams up with them to help them catch food, once chasing a mouse under the decking and swiping it in the opposite direction, into the jaws of the fox! Another client told me about her dog who had an irrational fear of seeing hot air balloons in the air; we have no idea why. However, she tends to know the exact weather conditions when air balloons will be out in force. On those days, she refuses to go on a walk.

Lastly, there are the clients that we like to see for much more superficial reasons - the good looking clients! Obviously if the animal is very unwell, we barely register how the client looks but if they are coming in for something routine, it can certainly brighten our day. I work in a very female dominated profession so most of the time, those that are commented on are the good looking men and some names are known by the whole practice. You may get a sly smile from receptionists when they tell you your next client has arrived with a remark about how good a specimen the 'dog' is. I have even managed to go on a couple of dates with one of these clients after seeing his dog out of hours. He had the number for the 'out of hours' mobile phone and started messaging it, assuming it was my own phone. After a couple of weeks of conversation on my actual phone, we had a few dates and although it didn't work out, it was still an enjoyable few weeks and makes for a great story.

Another time I can remember is when there was a British bulldog giving birth to a litter of puppies. The owners were anxious and had heard a lot of stories of bulldogs needing C-sections so asked if they could sit in a room in the practice for a few hours during the birthing process. They were one of the most attractive families we'd ever seen, with two hunky sons and both parents gorgeous. The grandmother turned up at one point and even she still looked better than me. We kept sending members of staff down to the room to check that the whelping process was going to plan but we'd send a different vet or nurse down each time, just so they could all have a gawp. Very unprofessional we know, but it did no harm and certainly put a smile on all our faces! The bulldog delivered all the puppies naturally and was a great mother too.

Essentially, anyone who isn't nasty can be classed as a nice client. Just being a normal human who talks in a polite way to all members of staff is good enough for me. Those that you see regularly and build up a bond with are just that extra bit special. Now I have left, I am friends with a lot of my clients on social media so they can see what goes on with my life and message me some vetty questions from time to time. We do like to see the same, lovely clients repeatedly so if you do feel like you've formed a bond with a certain vet or nurse, please do ask to see that particular person again. It helps your pet with continuity of care, but often also brings us joy to know we are not just imagining these relationships that we are building! It is a compliment to any of us to want to be seen again by the same client as it means that we must be doing our job to a good level and making a difference to people's lives.

PUS

You know those people who actually liked squeezing spots when you were a teenager? Vets and vet nurses are those people. We generally love anything that we can lance, pop, squeeze or burst. Those who are squeamish, turn away now. If you're eating any food, I would stop.

When a cat is bitten by another cat, as so often happens in fights over territory, an abscess can form. This is because their teeth harbour so many different types of bacteria which are then plunged into the skin of the other cat. These abscesses sometimes need to be lanced. When a vet brings a cat with an abscess over to the nurses, there's generally a fight to see who can help us. We tend to clip a little patch of fur, clean the area and then use a scalpel blade to make a hole in the abscess. This is a moment of pain for the cat, but given the skin is usually under tension and causing discomfort, this pain soon subsides when the pus comes out and relieves the pressure. You have to make sure you get the majority of the pus out; milking the pus from inside the abscess, through the hole and into the outside world. This is a very satisfying thing to do, watching thick yellow pus coming out of a small hole. Am I grossing you out yet? There was one time when I saw an abscess on a cat's foot; stabbing into that abscess relieved such pressure that a fountain of pus came out! People may have seen videos of similar situations on the internet, something some people find repulsive and others get addicted to. Some cats are not so handleable and will have to be sedated to perform this process too. There is a theory that many of these abscesses will heal by themselves without antibiotics, once all the pus has been flushed out because the source of infection has been removed. This does seem to have been the case in a few instances, but in my experience an antibiotic course often has to be given further down the line.

There are a few cats that are repeat offenders at this particular crime and will have multiple abscesses throughout their lives. Unfortunately, there is not much you can do to stop this as it is in their nature to fight over territory. My best advice is to get a water pistol and shoot at them. Images are floating through my mind of cats blasted out of the way by a big force of water from a powerful water gun. Please don't got that far, just one that gets them soggy will suffice. Cats that aren't castrated have a much increased incidence of fighting as they will also be fighting over any females that aren't neutered that are in the area. Thus, neutering your cats will help reduce these battles. Feline leukaemia virus (FeLV) is transmitted by cat bites too, if the cat has the virus in their system. Leukaemia is a cancer of the white blood cells and bone marrow and in cats, can be caused by the leukaemia virus. Cats that have the virus can then have the cancer or at least a weakened immune system that makes them susceptible to other infections or conditions. It is something that we now routinely vaccinate against. Any cat that goes outside should be vaccinated against FeLV for its own sake and for the protection of any cats it may end up fighting with. Sorry to be boring, but I like to give some useful advice occasionally. Makes this all a bit more worthwhile than just my random word vomit splurged onto a page. As a side note, as much as we like pus, we actually don't like vomit or diarrhoea as that's a step too far. Or enemas. Recently I had to remove concrete-like faeces from the colon of a dog. He was exceedingly constipated due to eating a mix of bones and a load of hay from its bedding (confusing I know, given it's not a rabbit). The faeces was so stuck in the colon that

I had to use birthing forceps to remove it. That's right, I birthed the poo from its anus.

Anyway, back to things we actually do like. Full anal glands are something that a lot of dogs, and the occasional cat, suffer with. The anal glands are the scent glands either side of the rectum that release some of their secretion onto the faeces as it leaves the body. When dogs go around smelling each other's bottoms or faeces, this is what they are smelling. Sometimes, they get blocked either due to the faeces not being solid enough, just bad conformation, or very overweight dogs where there is a layer of fat around the gland. This is where we come in! We have to release the anal gland secretion by inserting our finger into the dog's rectum and milking the contents out the duct to the external world. Our lives are so glamorous. What did you do today? Oh you sat at a desk in your nice work dress and went for drinks afterwards? That's nice, I emptied three sets of anal glands and the last lot went in my hair. In dogs that have to have this done regularly, we often offer to teach the owner how to do it to save them money and trips in to the vets. This tends to be greeted by some disgusted looking faces, a look down at some false nails or a gagging response. It is probably the only thing that owners would actively prefer to pay for than do themselves. We do find it weirdly satisfying though, despite the smell that is a bit like rotten fish mixed with faeces.

Some animals have cysts on their body that rupture and express sebaceous material - white to brown, granular material. Occasionally, the hole is small and you can squeeze the secretion out and it comes out like a wiggly worm or toothpaste from a tube. I swear my mouth is watering just thinking of doing that - is that weird? Dogs will sometimes get blackheads which are fun to squeeze as well; the most amazing of these being a hairless Chinese crested dog who had them all over his back! How that lady got anything done and didn't just sit there squeezing her dog's blackheads is beyond me.

One of my colleagues had a particular thing about ear wax in pets too. If really dirty, it can be very satisfying to clean the fold in the ear with a cotton bud, bringing up big blobs of wax each time. If a dog has particularly hairy ears, we can pluck these whilst they are under sedation. When the ears are waxy at the same time as being hairy, you can pluck all the hair out in one solid mass of wax and hair, it coming out like a small candle! This hair and wax predisposes the dog to ear infections so is best to come out, plus it gives us such satisfaction to leave behind a clean, hairless ear canal.

Though it has to be said, the best of all disgusting things that occur in our jobs has to be the pyometra. A pyometra, or 'pyo', is a pus-filled womb which is as delightful as it sounds. If dogs are not neutered, they are at a 25% risk of getting one of these when they get older. They happen due to age-related cystic change within the womb itself, that then becomes infected due to ascending bacteria - something that can happen reasonably easily given dogs like to lick their own arseholes and then their vagina (why do I let dogs kiss me?) If the cervix is closed, the uterus gradually fills with pus, causing stomach cramps, a high temperature and toxins being spread throughout the blood stream, increasing thirst and making the dog nauseous. If left, the uterus can rupture within the abdominal cavity. I have seen this happen once and we managed to save the dog's life, despite bits of pus floating around in its abdomen.

When pyometras occur, it requires emergency surgery to remove the uterus, with a much bigger risk of bleeding because all the vessels are engorged and the tissue is much more friable. The anaesthetic risk is significantly higher too due to the effects the toxins have in the bloodstream. Pyometras are the main reason we encourage female dogs to be spayed at a younger age; we spay dogs a few months after a season, when the uterus is smallest, most tough and unlikely to bleed thus the risk of surgery is greatly reduced. Mammary tumours are also much more likely to occur in entire females. In large breed dogs over 20kg, please do wait until 12-18 months to spay your dog if possible as this reduces the risk of joint issues and bone tumours, and anecdotally reduces risk of urinary incontinence. In small breed dogs, there is no need to wait and we can even perform 'pre-season spays 'at 6 months old to avoid the hassle associated with having a bitch in season. However, if everyone spayed their dogs when they should, we would be deprived of the joy of 'popping the pyo'. We do this once the dog is fully awake and recovering well. The pyo is put within a bag so the nurses don't shout at us for getting mess everywhere. We lance the pyo like a large abscess and a whole load of pus comes out - the biggest one I have popped was 3kg. It is very gross to anyone outside of the medical world, but we do love it.

Having said all this, one of the vets and one of the nurses at my practice did not like anything with a bad smell so a particularly smelly, horrible abscess would set them both off retching and gagging. It is always very amusing to witness these two working together over such an abscess. They'll both be holding the animal whilst trying not to vomit, eyes streaming and trying to do the job at the same time. The same happens if either has to clear up some fetid faeces too, or a set of infected anal glands. It sometimes makes us all wonder how it didn't put either of them off being in this line of work.

The majority of us are particularly disgusting as a profession though and despite doing all these things, we can immediately go upstairs to eat our lunch, even if that lunch involves cream cheese..

VET NURSES

When we work as vets, we have a whole load of staff to help us do our jobs. When you first walk into a vets, you are likely to be greeted by a receptionist or two. They are the ones that book your appointments, take your orders for medication, answer your queries on the phone and in person, plus take payment for the goods or services you have received. There are also the administration staff working behind the scenes to facilitate the smooth running of the vet practice. These people all tend to make our lives as vets a bit easier, and give us less admin work to do and we very much appreciate everything they do. However, there is no member of staff that helps us more than the vet nurse. When I typed 'vet nurse', I envisaged some kind of harmonious, angel song and a bright light appearing before you as you read. If it didn't, let's try that again. The incredible VET NURSE. Ok, better. This chapter is basically a love letter to all the vet nurses out there. If you don't know much about them, please read on.

These are split into trainee nurses and Registered Veterinary Nurses (RVNs), usually some of these being 'senior', 'deputy head 'or 'head nurse'. To become an RVN you can go to university for 3-4 years or you can go to college one day a week and work in practice all the rest of the time as a trainee, which usually takes 2-3 years. There are multiple exams throughout the whole of both courses and the level to which they have to learn about animals is not too far from that of a vet. Any senior vet nurse that you speak to will be able to tell you all about common diseases of pet animals and can even give you treatment options - though they are not legally allowed to prescribe anything.

They have also entered into the veterinary profession due to their love of animals and are often far more astute to the levels of husbandry that an animal needs than a vet is. For example, we can put a sick cat in a kennel with a bed, food and water, work out what drugs it will need to get better and set out a treatment plan. This is all the animal will *need* to get better. What the nurses do is make life that little bit better and give them what they *want*. They go to get a box to put in the kennel for the cat to hide in to feel safe, they offer various foods of different varieties, warming some up in the microwave to improve the smell and sit there hand feeding them to try to tempt them. They are the ones who will sit and wipe the cat's face, give it an olbas oil steam to try and remove any discharge from around its nose and spray the kennel with a calming pheromone product. They look after them closely from day to day and can see any slight personality changes that may indicate that they are getting better or are in more pain that day. In this way, they are invaluable to us as vets.

When you're a recently qualified vet, the nurses are your lifeline. When you graduate, you possess all the knowledge and theory behind how to be a vet and you know how to diagnose and treat patients, often knowing more rare diagnoses and modern treatments than your older colleagues. However, you are lacking some vet life skills. The 'gold standard' way of dealing with things is how you're taught at vet school but sometimes it may not be the best path for an animal or for the owner. Some nurses will have been qualified for longer than you will have been born. (Not a lie, we are twenty three or four when we graduate, most vet nurses over forty five will fit into this category. Feel old yet?) These nurses can give great advice on how to deal with a case and there are also certain practical skills at which they are better than you are - taking blood samples and emptying anal glands for example! Just knowing where everything is in the practice and how the computer system works can be a blessing. Even now, there are still times when one of the nurses will have an idea for a patient's care plan that I haven't thought of, or have a practical brainwave such as putting part of an empty syringe over the end of a tail that a dog keeps whacking against the wall and causing to bleed. They essentially have significantly more common sense than us vets! We are also terrible at looking for things. It's called the 'vet look 'and it means we don't see things that are about to slap us in the face. Nurses come along and pick up a bit of cotton wool and there it is.

All nurses, whether they are halfway through their training or recently qualified, also help us in many other ways. They can hold wiggly animals for us whilst we are looking in their ears or clipping their nails; nurses have this ability to hold animals in a way that keeps them still and calm (no, I don't mean that they smother them). They monitor the anaesthetics during operations and have to learn how each drug interacts with the body and how they may be able to fix any issues that arise. They are trained in CPR and emergency triage. They know how to position animals for x-rays and run all the tests in the lab including blood tests, urine and microscopy. They give all our inpatients their medication and take all the dogs out for walks several times a day. They call and take calls from owners and can put out certain medications for us, under guidance from the clinical records. They can perform certain surgical procedures for us such as small lump removals, stitch ups of wounds or some tooth extractions. They perform their own nurse consults such as post op checks, senior health assessments, weight clinics and nail clips. They tend to have to cover reception when they are short staffed and any nurses with more senior roles have to sort out rotas, answer emails, order in drugs and medical equipment and be responsible for the running of the nursing team. We can be running behind on consults, knowing we have another few

to do and that we are keeping people waiting and then we realise that the pet we are currently examining needs a blood test
or needs to be admitted for a drip. In this situation, we can take
the animal out the back and hand them over to the nurses to do
these things for us. They manage to do all these things whilst
also keeping the vet practice clean and clearing up after the mess
that animals (and vets!) make. Thus, they are often as busy or
even busier than the vets are.

Due to all of this, it therefore makes me very angry when they
are treated badly by clients. Many times, we have had situations
where a trainee nurse has been sent away by a client, saying that
'she doesn't know what she's talking about, she's only a trainee;
get me someone who knows more'. Firstly, that trainee probably
knows more than most members of the public, regardless of
what that member of the public thinks. Secondly, that is never
a way to speak to anyone, especially as whatever the problem is,
it is unlikely to be their fault. Saying that you accept their advice and you appreciate their help but that you're very worried
about your animal and is there any chance they could go and
check that with someone else, would be a much nicer way of
phrasing things. Often trainee nurses are reduced to tears by a
client's words, especially those with intimidating personalities.
Unfortunately, even the older, most experienced nurses will still
be looked down upon by certain people in the world as 'just a
nurse'. The receptionists also get this treatment; being shouted
at and told they will only speak to or take advice from a vet.
When they then get into our consult room or get to speak to us
on the phone, they are often nice as pie and think we deserve to
be spoken to with some respect. Why they don't think that of all
members of staff is beyond me. There are obviously the few that
also speak to us vets like we are nothing more than something
they found on their shoe, but that's another story.

As well as the clients, there are sadly a few vets that can get a bit
grumpy with nurses when they are stressed too. In my opinion,

this is also unacceptable. Luckily, it was not too prevalent at my first practice. No matter how stressed you are or how bad a day you are having, it is unlikely that the nurse is voluntarily forgetting to give an inpatient its medication or run that blood sample you asked for. It is far more likely that they are also having a very busy time and it just happened to slip their mind in amongst all the other things they were planning on doing. Again, there are times when maybe we do need a more experienced nurse to hold a particularly angry cat or we really do need that certain instrument pretty quickly, but getting irate with the nurses or saying things in a deliberately nasty way is never going to make the situation better. The nurses are generally a ready made friendship group for any vet entering a practice. Many of my friends from my first practice are nurses, some of whom have left the practice and work elsewhere, but we all have so much in common and share the same sense of humour (more on that later) that we continue to meet up regularly to chat about life and our respective jobs. So if all vets could treat nurses as their friends and equals, then maybe a lot of vet practices would be happier places to work.

Nurses are also opened to be sued and can face these worries too. Some people think that the final responsibility lies with the vet and if we are present, this is true. However, if a nurse is in charge of a patient then they are the ones who are open to any complaints and legal action if necessary. One of my nurse colleagues had to go through weeks of worry after a client complained about a mix up with the cremation of her pet. As soon as a mistake was realised, the issue was sorted and no harm or damage was done. The human error was made purely because it was a terribly busy day and the nurse forgot to make a mark on a board for the cremation service. Obviously, we are always keen for any member of medical staff that consistently makes bad mistakes to be investigated but this was a nurse who was normally very conscientious and hard-working which the particular client knew only too well. To have this level of responsibility for their career means that nurses also require professional indemnity insurance.

The reason I am singling out nurses amongst the support staff more than the fantastic receptionists, animal care assistants, practice managers and admin staff is the fact that they never seem to get recognition for what they do. The public is probably unaware of just how much they do for us and for their pets but also as to how little pay they get. The average starting salary after 2-4 years of training is around £18,000 per year with a career high, on average, of about £28,875 (for comparison, human nurses get on average, a fully deserved £33,385). Given the list of jobs they are required to be able to do, the level of knowledge that they have, the stress they have to go through and the hours that they have to work, this is pretty abysmal. Most nurses have different shifts on each day of the week, usually nine or ten hour days, with a one hour, unpaid lunch break. There is then a weekend rota that they have to take part in, with at least Saturday mornings worked and usually full weekend days worked too, occasionally luckily 1 in 7 or 8, sometimes as often as 1 in 3 full weekends. Those that work in practices with their own on call or inpatient care will then have to take part in out of hours or 'on call 'rotas too with all of these nurses having to sign out of the 48 hour week 'maximum'. There may be overtime paid or extra pay for nurses that are called out when on call, but I know many practices where this is not the case. How can a profession that has to be trained in so much, and know so much, be so underpaid and undervalued for the amazing job that they do? Outside of nursing, the general average salary in the UK, is £29,600 a year. Go back and read the vet nurse salaries again and see if you think that that is fair. There are no vet nurse unions to fight for higher salaries so most nurses do the job for the love of the animals and the sense of job satisfaction. There is no way of increasing their salaries whilst vet care is already considered to be 'expensive 'and we 'feel bad 'charging for nurse consults and nurse time so there is no obvious way out of all of this. At least by writing this, I hope all the nurses realise how much a lot of us appreciate everything they do and that the public can see what a tough job they have.

PUPPIES AND KITTENS

No matter how long you have been a vet for, you still love to see puppies and kittens for their first consults. There are some that are cuter than others of course, but we pretty much like seeing all of them. We definitely like to cuddle them and talk to them in a silly voice whilst we are also examining them. It is such a happy time for owners to get a new pet or even a first pet and we love being a part of that. Puppies often have a particular sweet smell to them and most of them don't have any fear of the vet so we get all the cuddles and kisses we want! Sometimes, we will have a whole litter of puppies booked in for their first vaccines and that is a fabulous way to spend half an hour of our day. Though when they are travel sick and come in covered in their own vomit and excrement, I suppose they are a bit less cute.

People often ask us which breeds to get or what advice we give to owners so here is a very quick guide to what we like the most.

Firstly, no matter which puppy or kitten you have there are some easy tips to make your vet's life more simple in the future. Gently putting your fingers in their ears and giving them a wiggle will mean that if they need ear drops in the future, they aren't immediately freaked out. The same thing can be said for looking at their feet and teeth. Plus, if you want to bring some nail clippers close to their nails and mimic clipping them, that may also help; we can show you how to do it for real if you're scared. Teeth brushing from a young age can get them used to it and reduce the need for dental procedures in the future.

We would also advise never having your puppy or kitten sleeping in the same room as you, even for one or two nights to 'settle them in'. You can change your mind in the future but if you start at the beginning, you will struggle to get them back out again. I once had a double puppy consult with two sisters who had just picked up their Jack Russell puppies and brought them straight to us for a check over. They lived separately, but wanted their dogs to be friends from the start so thought it was easiest to get siblings. One of them remarked that they were going to get a crate and put them in the bedroom for the first few nights; her sister said she didn't think that was a good idea and asked for my advice. Our advice is always to crate them or put them in a small room, with a bed and some toys and create a 'safe space' for them to be. We ask owners to put them in there to go to sleep, to go to bed themselves and put some earplugs in and ignore any whining. It may go on for quite a while but they should eventually stop. They have just gone from being surrounded by their mother and their siblings to being alone at night - it may sound very mean to leave them but if you go down to them, they will learn by the end of the night that they only have to cry to get your attention. It may be a good idea to have given the neighbours some wine as an apology for the first few nights! I have heard a few stories of puppies that whine for hours and hours with the owners just getting increasingly frustrated and worried about neighbours but this is very rare and persistence for several nights does eventually cause them to stop.

A couple of weeks later, the sisters returned for their second vaccination and I asked how they were getting on. The sister who had listened to our advice had a well behaved puppy who could sleep through the night and was happy to be left alone for a couple of hours in the daytime too. The other sister looked knackered and said she thought she had the badly behaved puppy but turns out she had not taken our advice and had slept with the puppy in her room. The puppy had continued to cry so much that she had taken her out of her crate and put her in the bed with her. Thus, the puppy would sleep for a couple of hours and then wake up, want to play with her mummy and not let her sleep for 45 mins until she'd had her playtime and would settle for another couple of hours. This extended to the daytime too - howling when the owner would leave the house and it meant that they hadn't been separated for more than a quick food shop for the previous two weeks.

Unfortunately, this type of behaviour becomes ingrained very rapidly and it took a lot of training to allow her owner to lead a more normal life again. It does make things much more difficult for us as vets too as these dogs turn out to be very spoilt and don't want anything done to them that they don't agree with. Thus taking blood tests or putting IV lines in become virtually impossible and even simple nail clips can be a challenge, let alone a stay in the hospital overnight if they ever become ill. The same theory can be applied to kittens - but they are much less trainable! We would still very much recommend that you try to train them to sleep apart from you to start with, even if you change your mind in the future.

Secondly, actually picking a puppy or kitten to start with can be a challenge. There are the simple rules that everyone should follow to reduce the puppy and kitten farming business. Always ask to see the mum of the litter. A breeder should always have the mother nearby; if they cannot show you the mother, walk away. Unless your pet is the last one in the litter, you should be able to meet the siblings too. You should go to the place that the dog is kept, certainly not 'meet halfway 'in the back of a car or van, unless you have been to see the pups previously. The breeder should also have vaccination information on the parents of the litter; if the mother has not been vaccinated, your puppy or kitten may not have any maternal antibodies in its blood stream and is more likely to develop conditions that we vaccinate against before it can be vaccinated itself. This is especially true for kittens and cat flu; unfortunately, once a kitten has cat flu, a vaccination won't stop it having the condition for life. It is also advisable to ask your puppy to have had a vet check and relevant paperwork to say so. If they have had their first vaccination, then documents for this will be enough.

With kittens, it is unfortunately less common for this to be done but if you are buying an expensive pedigree breed, we would still suggest it happens. Puppies over 8 weeks old are legally supposed to be microchipped, with relevant documentation. You should also check if any puppy or kitten has had flea and worming treatment. There are many times when people bring in a puppy or kitten that is in poor condition and they tell us that they had to take it because they couldn't bear to leave it in that environment. Sadly, this is what irresponsible breeders and puppy farms sometimes rely on, and you are still giving them your money and funding more animals to be treated in the same way. Heartbreaking as it is, if you suspect any cruelty, walk away, call the RSCPA and continue the search for your own pet. This is particularly true for any litters that you see with cropped ears - this is illegal in the UK and barbaric. Anyone who performs this act should be reported straight to the police. Tail docking and dew claw removal should have certification to say it has been performed by a vet under a quick anaesthetic and that it is only done because the dogs are going to be working so more likely to rip the dewclaws or tails. Ear cropping has no medical benefit and is never done by a vet; would you like your ears cut off whilst conscious?

We always like to hear that people have done their research on a certain breed and that they know what they are getting themselves in for. There are always certain breeds that we would tend to avoid as vets, though that doesn't mean that they don't have their own merits. For example, French bulldogs have become increasingly popular over the past few years due to their amazing personalities and friendly nature. They are the very definition of 'ugly cute', along with pugs and British bulldogs because of their flat faces, known as 'brachycephalic'. Unfortunately, they have been bred so quickly and the same lines used over and over again, meaning that they estimate 50% of them now have skin allergies. This may seem minor at first glance, but when you have a dog with skin allergies, you start to see how miserable it makes their life. They constantly chew at their paws, get recurrent ear infections and skin infections and it soon starts to make them irritable because, well, wouldn't you be if you constantly had an itch that you couldn't get rid of? We can use various treatments to improve their quality of life but unfortunately, there is no magic wand that we can wave to cure the issue. It is a consistent battle with regular medication and trips to the vets and even then, they can still get flare ups. Given most of the drugs we use are there to stop their extreme immune system overreacting to allergens, they are expensive and over a long period of time, may have deleterious effects on the health of the animal, depending on the drug. On top of this, Frenchies, pugs and bulldogs also have Brachycephalic Obstructive Airway Syndrome (BOAS), meaning that they have very enclosed nostrils, a long soft palate that obstructs their throat, extra tissue that grows at the back of their throat and a very narrow windpipe. All these things together mean that they make what people think are adorable sniffy, snorting noises and will snore a lot of the time. However, it is a pretty awful way to live! Try narrowing your nostrils by about half and try to breathe through them. Bit of a struggle isn't it? And that's without all the other issues at the back of the throat.

In milder cases, they just learn to live with it and accept that this is how life is and can be very happy. In more extreme cases, they will not be able to walk very far, especially in hot weather; they will vomit regularly due to the pressure in their airways pulling their stomach into their chest cavity (hiatus hernia), they can inhale their own saliva and get a type of pneumonia, and unfortunately, can drop dead at any moment. One particularly hot weekend that I was on call, I had two British bulldogs from two different families brought in to me for cremation because they collapsed on a walk and died there and then. Both of them were 5-6 years old. This tragedy can be helped by BOAS surgery to improve their breathing, but it can be a risky surgery and costs a lot of money. Sadly, their health issues don't stop there. Lots of the brachycephalic breeds also have malformed backbones, meaning that they easily get issues with their spinal cord and can experience back pain, slipped discs and paralysis. Their legs are often wonky too, with out-turned elbows and wrists. Still thinking of getting one? That's fine, but please try to find a breeder who is mating lines that have longer noses, wider nostrils, no skin issues and well-formed legs. They do exist and vets very much like it when these are the puppies we see! We are sick of seeing breeders who don't care about breeding healthy versions of these dogs; they see it as a fast way to make money and don't care that they are breeding more and more dogs that have severe health issues. They virtually always need a C-section too which is a lot to put a dog through more than once and it doesn't always go smoothly.

There are other breeds of dog that we would advise steering clear of - German shepherds and Sharpeis being the next two that come to mind. When we learn about conditions that dogs can get, we have a list of 'predisposed breeds 'to that certain condition. German Shepherds are on the list for quite a lot of these conditions; far more than any other breed. They can also be quite neurotic due to their high intellect and need to expend energy, along with anything Husky related. So for these breeds, you need to be prepared to do a lot of exercise and mental stimulation! Sharpeis have very wrinkly skin and the majority of them have constant skin infections, ear infections and sore eyes due to their eyelids rubbing on the surface of the eyes. A lot of Sharpei puppies have 'tacking 'surgery when very young puppies, under a quick anaesthetic, to evert their eyelids to try to prevent this from happening, just to give them a chance at normal eye function and reduce this chronic source of pain. Sadly, due to these issues and likely with some interference with genetics too, a lot of Sharpeis become very aggressive and if you ask any vet what their thoughts are when they see a Sharpei booked into see them, it will be that they will need a muzzle. Far more than any Rottweiler or Dobermann - the type of dogs that people tend to think of as aggressive.

Dachshunds (or sausage dogs) have very long backs and malformed legs and are very prone to slipping discs in their backs and needing spinal surgery to fix them; some dogs go on to have this occur more than once and can become paralysed. They quite commonly have 'small dog syndrome 'and can be quite snappy too if not socialised properly and are too pampered - similar to Chihuahuas. So if you would like a sausage dog, be prepared for the possibility of a very large bill from a spinal surgeon and please socialise it a lot! Cavalier King Charles Spaniels, or 'cavvies 'are the most adorable and well-natured dogs, with their big googly eyes. Unfortunately, they are very prone to a certain heart condition that causes them to go into heart failure and pass away at a much younger age than would be normal for their size. We are happy if we see a cavvie over the age of 10! Responsible breeders are trying to breed out the condition as much as possible but the problem is that heart murmurs often don't become apparent until 5-6 years of age when the bitch has already had a litter or two of puppies. If you do your research and find a breeder who has bred a couple of generations of cavvies who don't go on to develop heart disease, then this may be your best bet.

Unfortunately, if you wanted a list of every dog breed that is predisposed to something bad then it would mean there wouldn't be many breeds left to choose from! Flat coat retrievers and boxers are prone to certain cancers; giant breeds like Great Danes and Irish wolfhounds are prone to heart disease, particular cancers and most pass away before the age of 8; Labradors are more likely to get hip and elbow dysplasia and thus arthritis from a very early age; poodles can get Addison's disease; westies can get terrible skin disease; Rottweilers are prone to bone tumours; the list goes on. The main advice we can give is to research the breeder and ask about any steps they have taken to try to reduce the risk of your puppy developing those particular issues that are related to the breed.

A quick note on hypoallergenic dogs; anything that is crossed with a poodle can claim to be hypoallergenic so that people who suffer from allergies to dogs may be able to cope with them. However, in reality only about 50% of these are actually hypoallergenic and don't shed fur. So please bear this in mind when picking a puppy - there are rising numbers of these types of dogs in rescue homes due to this issue.

With cats, it is a lot easier. The healthiest breeds are the domestic 'moggy 'cats - the majority of cats in the UK. Some of the longer haired breeds are obviously more prone to furballs and shedding so this may influence your decision! Any pedigree breed is more prone to genetic disease due to the inbreeding that occurs in some lines, even if some breeders are trying to be more responsible now. Persian cats are similar to the brachycephalic dogs like bulldogs - they often struggle to breathe and can get chronic nasal discharge and infections. Their eyes are more bulbous and prone to conjunctivitis and ulceration. They also have hereditary kidney issues - something that can sadly cause kidney failure at a young age. Maine Coon and Norwegian forest cats can be very large, like small tigers! Unfortunately, that comes with a type of genetic heart disease where the walls of the heart become thickened and can dramatically shorten their lives. For all these breeds, there are responsible breeders out there trying to test for these conditions and only use healthy animals, so please do your research before you buy one of these kittens.

All pedigree breeds of cat are more prone to a disease called FIP (Feline Infectious Peritonitis), a fatal disease that affects the cat at a very young age. It is a caused by a virus that is prevalent throughout the cat population but it randomly mutates inside some cats to give FIP. We still don't know the reason why pedigree breeds are more prone to the condition but we know that multi-cat households are more likely to cause the mutation, through stress and virus load. Therefore, a breeder that only has a couple of cats, or keeps the cats separate, is less likely to have a kitten that develops the condition. It is still a rare condition and unfortunately a lot of the time it is just bad luck. The only other note about picking a kitten is that there are a great number of 'pedigree cross 'breeds out there that people pay quite a bit of money for. When they come in to see us as vets, a lot of the time they are just 'moggy 'cats who the owners have been tricked into paying more for! Please be aware of this and ask to physically see the parents, not just photos, or ask that the kittens have a vet check before you buy and get some paperwork from the vet that can confirm the cross-breed status.

Having said all this, no matter what goes on to happen in a pet's life and no matter what the breed is, seeing a puppy or a kitten never does get old! We may dread what will happen to that pet in the future or worry about the welfare of the place it came from, but looking at those puppy dog eyes or hearing the tiny meow from a kitten will never stop being one of the best parts of our job.

PEOPLE WHO SAY
WE ARE GOOD
VALUE FOR MONEY

Here's another chapter without funny animal stories; I promise we will get back to those next time.

The majority of the time, people are complaining about their bill (literally *every day*) but we get probably one client a month that comes in to see us and remarks that the bill is much cheaper that they expected. We very much like these people. They tend to be doctors, dentists or Americans. In America, they are used to paying for their own healthcare as well as their pet's care. Veterinary services cost a lot more in America than they do here, so Americans are delighted to pay our prices. Doctors and dentists will know the cost of services to the NHS and know that we charge a lot less than this in certain instances. A doctor once told me that surgery on the NHS costs £100 a minute. So when you go in to have your leg fracture repaired and it takes a few hours, that's £12-18,000 of care you've received, not including the stay in hospital after and the painkillers. A simple fracture repair for your cat would cost about £1,000-2,000 including overnight care and ongoing drugs. If it was more complex and had to be referred to a specialist orthopaedic surgeon, your bill may reach £6-7,000; still a fraction of the price of human care, for the same level of skillset.

Following on from the previous chapter about vet nurse salaries and how things can be changed, I wondered whether many people may be thinking that vets earn so much money that we should take a pay cut and give some to the nurses. Well I would like to dispel that myth as much as I can for you now. Firstly, to explain why we deserve the salaries we get and that those salaries aren't as high as you think they may be. Secondly, to breakdown the costs of the care that you receive and why we charge what we do.

So here are the stats: the average salary for a GP veterinary surgeon in the UK is around £46,400 a year, with a mean starting salary of £33,500 and an average high, for practice owners, of between £60-70,000 per annum. I'm not going to pretend that they are low salaries, I know we earn a decent living and that we are fortunate to have a job that pays well and is a safe job both now and in the future. We have a comfortable life and can afford to give our families most of the things they need and more. *However*, let us compare these salaries to those of doctors and dentists who are 'equivalents 'in terms of debt and training before the start of the job. The salaries for these occupations are standardised by the NHS so start at just over £28,000 and, once a qualified GP after about another six or seven years, earn around £60,000 with a maximum of £91,000 over a career. The rates are very similar for NHS dentists. Specialist vets who go on to do further training and work in referral hospitals get paid significantly more, just like consultant doctors or dentists. However, most people talking about vets being expensive are referring to us GP vets.

There is a lot of work that goes into being a vet; probably far more than the public realises as the work begins far before going to university. GP vets have started off their training when young teenagers, deciding they want to enter into the profession. At this point, we are told that the competition for vet school is *very* high and that we will need to have done some work experience prior to application to university, in order to receive an offer of a place. We then start to give up time after school in order to gain this experience. I spent every Friday evening for a few months at a dairy farm learning cow handling and the milking process. For about six months, I spent my Saturday mornings at the local wildlife hospital. I did a couple of weeks' work experience within a small animal practice, making sure I was comfortable watching operations and witnessing euthanasias. I even spent a morning in a slaughterhouse to show my dedication to the job, as many vets are meat and health inspectors in abattoirs. This was all before the age of seventeen when I applied to four vet schools. Most of the vets I know had done similar levels of work experience. This is on top of the studying for top grades at GCSE and A-level.

When we get to university, it is a five or six year course depending on the university you go to. This is the same for doctors, with dentistry being four years. Within our university holidays, we have to complete 12 weeks of animal handling work experience in the first 2 years, with 26 weeks of clinical work experience in the last 3 years, shadowing vets in a mixture of small animal, farm animal and equine practice. The majority of this is, of course, unpaid because we aren't exactly useful, just there to witness the job and learn how certain things are treated in practice. It does, however, stop us from getting *actual* jobs in the university holidays and we do incur costs in terms of petrol. Again, this is on top of studying for our exams, of which we have many; one of my friends counted - 57 exams in total. Veterinary medicine is consistently voted in as one of the hardest courses in the country, along with medicine of course.

Then there's the debt we rack up whilst studying at university. The tuition fees alone now that the fees are £9,000 a year, will add up to £45,000 for a five year course, or £54,000 for the six years. That's not including any maintenance loans, or the costs of accommodation and expenses for the time we are there. Don't get me wrong, I wouldn't trade my university experience for anything, but the fact that I've got so much debt to pay back, especially with the interest gained every year, is a constant niggle on my finances.

When we enter the job, we act as GPs taking consults with clients; we then do our own blood tests, urine tests, needle biopsies and sometimes x-rays and ultrasounds, right there and then. We know how to interpret all these tests to varying levels, with some of us being better at some things than others. We perform routine surgical procedures such as neutering and lump removals, along with more complex surgical and emergency procedures. We are dentists too, knowing how to extract even the most difficult of teeth and some vets know how to perform root canals and crowns too. We have own versions of ICU, various wards and isolation rooms for infectious cases. One of my doctor friends was amazed to learn that one vet can perform such a range of skills. I told her of the time I had a middle-aged Labrador come to see me for sudden onset lethargy; I examined the animal, knew from that to perform an ultrasound of its abdomen and found a bleeding tumour on its spleen. It required urgent stabilisation and surgery to remove that mass and along with the nurse, got it through said surgery and looked after it for the rest of the day and gave it all the drugs it needed to combat any after effects of the surgery. This is something any experienced vet can do by the way, I'm not some animal saviour. She estimated that about five different doctors and a whole team of nurses would have been involved in the equivalent in human medicine.

We also have very long working hours and stressful working conditions. Our job is *literally* a matter of life or death in some circumstances, with a lot of pressure on our shoulders. We often have to do on call shifts or overnight care along with working full days too. Whenever we have to make plans at the weekend, we always have to consult our weekend rota to see whether we have to miss that particular gathering or not. It goes without saying that we also have to sign out of the 48 hour maximum working week. We obviously have to work on difficult cases, trying to figure out what is wrong with an animal when it is something more abnormal, which plays on our mind throughout the day and in the middle of the night too. We often work over any lunch breaks, or stay late in the evenings if emergencies come down or if we have many sets of blood results to report before we go home. Outside of work, each vet has to complete *35 hours* of Continuing Professional Developing (CPD) per year to learn about the latest techniques and drug within vet medicine.

We don't get many perks to the job either. I have a lot of friends that aren't vets who receive perks such as great pensions, private medical care, limitless sick pay, extended holiday pay and great maternity packages. Some friends are signed up to services through their job that give them money off at restaurants, free cinema tickets, free access to some exercise apps and websites. As vets, especially those working in independent practices though most of the time in corporate practices too, we get just 5 days a year of paid sick leave, 4 weeks of holiday, and only statutory maternity pay. We receive the workplace pension and it's up to us to save more if we can, unlike the fantastic NHS pension. Some farm animal vets will get vehicles provided to them given the amount of driving they have to do for work, but their pay is lessened accordingly. We rely upon having generous bosses for any extras such as team bonding days out, Christmas parties and Easter eggs! I don't want you to get the violins out, we know what we sign up for and it is the same with a lot of other jobs.

Now don't get me wrong, I think doctors deserve every penny they get and more. They have all the studying, debt and stress that we have but with humans instead of animals. I know that a lot of people joke to us that they'd rather a family member died than their beloved pet, but *how* doctors cope with the stress of saving a human life or having to break bad news to people and families about their health is beyond me. They do an incredible job, as do dentists, but we also do a very good job in our area of medicine. As you can see from the figures above, all of us start our careers just above the national UK average salary, after doing all the studying and extra work we've done. Given the lack of confidence that most of us have at the start of our career, and given this is so much more money than any of us have ever seen, we are certainly happy with that! As the years go by, doctors 'and dentists 'salaries rise at a steady rate to a level many thousands above that of vets. We can never hope to achieve the money that they can earn, let alone the money that some of my friends outside of veterinary medicine make. Their jobs obviously require high levels of intelligence and have stress in their own way, but they do not have the pressure of another life on their shoulders, and most of them don't have to work weekends! I recently told one of my friends who works in finance about my sick leave and maternity package and she was genuinely shocked. I know the majority of jobs in the UK will have the same lack of benefits as us, and that many jobs have weekend rotas and night shifts, but I imagine these people don't have comments made daily about how 'they earn so much'. You can now see that we do earn decent wages but it is, in my opinion, fully deserved for the job we do. I don't hear many people complaining that doctors get paid too much (which they definitely don't!), despite them getting paid significantly more than us.

So now we've talked about our own salaries, how about I explain where a lot of the costs go when you pay for something at the vets?

As with any business, we have to pay rent/mortgages on the buildings, utility bills, buying of computer and phone systems and their maintenance, costs of consumables and any upgrades to the buildings that are needed. On top of this we have the very expensive veterinary equipment to cover. When paying for a blood test, you are firstly paying for the skill of the vet and nurse, the syringes, blood tubes and needles. Then the bill has to cover the cost of the single-use slides that we put into the machine for every single blood test. Oh and that machine that we use? It costs £20-25,000. Thus, we slowly have to pay that off with every blood test we take. The same is true for any ultrasound your pet has to have. The machines vary in their image quality and you do get what you pay for; the one at my last practice cost around £25,000 which is on the upper end of those used in GP practices but it meant we could get more diagnoses for your pets and use it to take guided biopsies.

Endoscopes are used to look into the stomach, intestines, up the nose and even into the lungs; they can take biopsies or grab out something that shouldn't be there. The ones that attach to a camera screen cost around £10,000. As you can imagine, they have to be cleaned thoroughly between each animal with some specialised cleaning products too. The nurses don't tend to fight over who cleans that one!

Then you've got the X-ray machines and the cost of lining the room with lead for safety which is another £25-30,000. The dental machine along with specific dental X-ray can be another £5000, plus all the costs of the ongoing cleaning, handheld elevators and extractors. We, of course, have multiple anaesthetic machines at several thousand each, plus the cost of the oxygen and anaesthetic gas. We have the monitoring equipment that helps keep your pet safe whilst under the anaesthetic. Drip pumps to set the rate of fluids going into the pet's body cost around £1000 each and we need many of them as you can only use one per patient. Even our eye pressure machine cost about £1500 and we only use it once every few weeks when we think a pet has glaucoma! These are all significant extra costs that we have to cover and thus the costs of the investigative procedures and surgery have to account for this. Plus, we have to have all these machines serviced and their safety checked every year.

For those times when we have to send samples of lumps, faeces, blood, pus or urine to the laboratory, there are also more costs that we have to cover. Obviously, the lab themselves have their own price for the tests then we have to add on VAT, the cost of packaging and the courier to take the sample to the labs. For all these tests, we put about a 20% mark up on the costs in order to make a profit from them to pay for all the other things we need. Therefore, when you pay £100 for a lab test, only about £20 of it goes into the business bank account to go back to buying all the new equipment, bills and salaries.

Also, that CPD that we have to do 35 hours of every year? That also costs quite a bit of money for the practice. If we are sent to a day course that involves surgical practice as well as lectures, just that one day can be up to £1000. Just a series of lectures for the day costs the practice several hundred pounds. Some vets choose to do further qualifications called 'certificates 'to become partly specialised in a certain field within the job. Some of my friends are completing these now and they take at least 2 years, with costs ranging from £4500-10,000 depending on the company and subject. Then we all have to pay money to the Royal College of Veterinary Surgeons every year just for the privilege of being a vet or vet nurse. This year, those fees were £364 for vet, £71 for a nurse; some vet practices pay this for each vet or nurse that works there and some get you to pay it yourselves. We also have to have insurance for legal costs if someone tries to sue us - this is was £631 for the year for me as a locum so when a practice pays for multiple vets and nurses, the cost is certainly significant. Practices also pay for all the nurse college training and exam fees which adds up to over a couple of thousand for each nurse. You can see how these extra outgoings soon add up and why we have to charge more to cover them.

Another reason for costs of medicine being 'so high' is that our veterinary medicines are more expensive than the human counterpart. We have to administer drugs according to the 'cascade' which means that if a veterinary product exists, we have to use this drug; if it exists for a dog but not for a cat, that's our next port of call, and if there are no animal alternatives, only then can we legally prescribe human medicines. The drug manufacturers go through the licensing process to make a veterinary version of the human drugs, something which costs millions of pounds and years of work. For example, amlodipine is a human blood pressure medication that we can also use to treat cats with high blood pressure. A few years ago, one of the drug companies made a cat equivalent; exactly the same drug but a smaller dosage and more palatable to cats. Instead of using a quarter of a human tablet that cost a very small amount, we now have to use a whole tablet of the cat version, which is triple the price of the human one. This means that the amount we charge for the drug obviously has to triple too! This is not our choice, it is our licensing protocol and something we have to follow.

We are also certainly not in the pockets of the drug companies as so many people like to insist - we get no benefits from choosing a certain drug company as all our drugs come through a wholesaler anyway, who also have their mark up on the drugs. The only situation in practice nowadays where we get anything for free from the big drug companies is when the drugs reps will come into the vet surgery to deliver a 'Lunch and Learn' to all the vets and sometimes the nurses too. This is their opportunity to tell us about the latest drug that they have made a license for, or manufactured from scratch, trying to persuade us to use it. One of my boss's favourite activities was to ask difficult questions or pick holes in their studies, just to really make sure that the drug is as good as they said it was. In these situations, the drugs company will buy us free sandwiches, crisps and cakes. The majority of the time, a couple of staff members are left behind dealing with an emergency or long operation so they miss the presentation but do still get the free lunch!

The online pharmacies can get the drugs in at a much lower

price because they buy in bulk. We went through about twenty or thirty packs of flea treatment for cats in a day across four branches so this is the amount that we order in. Online pharmacies can order in thousands of packs a day so they get a discount for bulk buying. They don't have the overhead costs that we have and they can keep the drugs in warehouses with no real control on temperature or humidity so can afford to charge far less for the products. It is many pounds cheaper for me to buy flea treatment for my cat online than it was for me to get it from work, and we can get it for cost price from the wholesaler. So again, this is something we don't have too much control over. When we prescribe drugs in the practice, it is also including the cost of the prescription, rather like you pay for a prescription when getting drugs for yourself on the NHS. Therefore, we have to write you a prescription to get the drugs online, something that ranges from £10-20 depending on the practice and lasts for 3-12 months, so factor this in to the costs too. I certainly have no problem doing these written prescriptions for people and I actively suggest it when I know that pets are going to being on expensive drugs long term.

Unfortunately, I cannot pretend that all vets and businesses share the same ethics when it comes to pricing of the care of animals as my first practice did. I know there are stories of costs being far higher than they should be for certain situations - something I see whilst locuming. Each practice choses to make their profits in different places; some practices will put higher mark up on drugs and diagnostic tests, others put it on the surgery or anaesthetic fees. In contrast, they will have lower prices for consults, routine care and 'pet health clubs'. In some places, the overall costs are much higher altogether. This can be due to the location of the vet practice within the country or within the actual town itself; central buildings have higher rent, as do those in or near London. One practice I have locumed at had to charge more to compensate for the fact that the practice had £54,000 of debt from clients not paying their bills. Therefore, the new clients suffered due to the errors of previous clients.

Dedicated night-time vets are often more expensive due to the salaries of veterinary surgeons and nurses being about £8-10,000 higher than the average for day-time vets. This is obviously as an incentive to choose to work night shifts, rather than day shifts as specific emergency night-time vets don't tend to open during the day. The staff there tend to work 4-7 night shifts in a row - something most people wouldn't choose to do. Rather like calling a plumber out in the middle of the night or on a Sunday will cost you more than normal rates, you expect to pay more for vet care at these times. An ambulance call out in 2015-16 cost, on average, £270 to the NHS. Dedicated emergency vets are akin to you going into your nearest A&E, or an ambulance bringing you into the hospital and their fees are very similar to, or sometimes much less than that. The level of care that some of these places provide is outstanding and their experience with critical care medicine is higher than a lot of day-time practices and these higher fees are fully deserved. There are a few times that I've heard of when patients are stable, just need to be in on a drip and have some IV medication when these fees do seem higher than they should be. This is purely for the privilege of having a vet and a vet nurse on site, watching over your animal for the whole time like they are in the daytime.

A lot of practices, my first practice included, will keep stable patients in their own hospital overnight with checks until 10pm and a nurse in the building until the morning. They will come down to check on the patient if the drip pump beeps or she hears any disturbance. However, some practices do not have the licensing or the staff to be able to do this and their only option is to transfer these pets to an overnight service provider and have the higher fees charged. In this situation, it is important to remember that the vets and vet nurses that are watching over your pet overnight really are providing gold standard treatment. Certainly, if your pet is in an unstable position, this is the place where you would want it to be for the overnight care.

Also, it is worth remembering that it is never the individual vet, nurse or receptionist that is setting the prices in these places and getting angry at them for the cost of care isn't going to get you anywhere. If you truly feel overcharged, please go through the complaints procedure by writing an email or letter to the appropriate person. Vets are as keen as you are to stop practices that overcharge from working and bringing the reputation of the profession down. When choosing a vet practice for your pet, it may be worth asking what happens with the care of any overnight patients, and how much certain investigative procedures cost, rather than just relying on the price of a vaccine or a spay. Some practices will lure clients in with cheaper routine healthcare and you obviously hope this is all you will need in your pet's life. However, if your pet does become poorly, these practices will then charge much higher fees for all the blood tests, imaging, hospitalisation, surgery and drugs to make up for the money lost by the cheaper routine care. Often these costs will far outweigh the extra few pounds that it costs for a vaccination or the extra fifty pounds for a bitch spay at other practices.

Having said this, the majority of practices will price things fairly and it reflects the hard work we have all done to get to where we are. At the end of the day, we have to make a profit and we are also a business. An NHS consult for a GP costs about £30 for the NHS, but that's because they don't have to make a profit; a private GP appointment is about £70 because you can get an appointment whenever you would like it, within reason - something that we also try to achieve. A vet consult costs between £35 and £50 depending on the vet practice and location.

If we charged any less, we wouldn't be able to make a profit, recruit staff to do the job we do and there would be nobody here to look after your pets. So please, please take a leaf out of the book of those that remark in a positive way about the costs of our healthcare for your animals. Is a bill for £3000 in the middle of the night on a Saturday to save your dogs life with major surgery really 'extortionate'? Or the £1000 for a two day stay in hospital for your cat who ate some lilies which could cause her to go into kidney failure and die? Or indeed, the £50 a month you pay for your old dog with arthritis to have pain relief for the last couple of years of his life? Please think about the work it has taken all of us to get to where we are, and how much stress we are under day to day. I hope that you can now see why the costs are what they are. Someone recently talked about sending people home at the end of their visit to the NHS with a breakdown of costs so they can see what resources they have used. The thought was to try to reduce time wasters who go to the doctors for no reason or even miss appointments. I think it wasn't taken further for fears of people then feeling guilty about using the public money but it would certainly have helped us out. If someone wants to create an NHS for animals, please be my guest - it would make our lives a lot easier.

PETS DOING SILLY THINGS

Hurrah! A chapter that's not whingey.

We've all watched those silly videos of a vast array of different animals doing amusing things online or witnessed it ourselves at home with our pets. Luckily for me, this can sometimes be a daily occurrence in the normal life of a vet. We often have the excited dogs that come in to consults, tails wagging so hard their bottom wags too. Some of them will even 'smile', showing all their teeth and looking like they are snarling but they are, in fact, smiling. A few will even spring on their back legs like pogo sticks.

Pets that are in kennels with us can do a whole manner of amusing actions too. Any cats that are in for routine neutering tend to turn from hiding and scared pre-op into these adorable, mushy kitties after their op. This is the effect of the drugs we give and it is great to be able to interact with cats who just want to play and purr at you within the kennel. They will throw themselves down onto their sides or back in greeting, as cats bizarrely seem to do without hurting themselves. The only thing is that they will lie against the door, generally upside down and paws trying to bat your hand as you open said door. This means they will often fall out of the kennel as we open the door and we have to be ready to catch them. Others will be climbing up the doors that have bars across and trying to get your attention in any way they can. This all wears off after a few hours and they go home again. Luckily, dogs don't tend to go the same way with the drugs. I'm now imagining a Labrador trying to climb out of one of our kennels. We actually did have one very silly dog who managed to slip out of his (far too loose and pointless) collar when getting him out the kennel. He went through the main door into kennels as a nurse happened to be walking through it at the time. Then a vet just happened to be coming in through the main door of the building and... the dog was off on its great escape. Funny now we look back, *not* so funny at the time as various vets and nurses set off on a recapture mission through town. Needless to say, we now have a protocol that requires slip leads to be put on all dogs. Oh, the dog was fine by the way; he just didn't take kindly to being starved that morning for his procedure so had gone on a rampage to find food off any members of the public he came across.

My colleague had an escaped hamster in his consult room once and we had to keep the door closed all day and put a humane mouse trap out for it. Then there was the case of the mysterious, disappearing cat. We are used to cats trying to jump onto the highest place in the room or into the sink but this one managed to outwit both vet and owner by vanishing into thin air. This time, we had to leave some food and water out overnight and hope it came back out from Narnia. It did, but we still don't know where exactly it went for that time. Some of my friends have similar stories; cats stuck in the practice roof for a day and a cat that escaped from its basket in the carpark and managed to find its way to its home 7 miles away!

Then you have the animals who's silly behaviour gets them into trouble. These are the pets that eat objects that they shouldn't, causing a blockage in the intestines or stomach. The most notorious 'foreign body 'that we remove from dogs is a corn on the cob. The fibrous, solid middle is *not* digestible and is the perfect size to get stuck in the tube of the intestine. These dogs often present with sudden onset vomiting that does not stop, despite medical intervention. X-rays can sometimes show a very obvious, solid blockage but sometimes the signs are more subtle and we have to go off ultrasound or barium studies. If the blockage is not removed, usually via surgery, the piece of gut where the foreign body is stuck will die and the intestinal contents will seep into the abdomen, causing septic shock and death. As a practice, we removed dozens of these blockages and on top of all the socks, sofa cushions, towels and bits of toys, there are certainly a few more memorable moments. One particularly stupid mastiff decided to eat virtually an entire box of disposable gloves. A silly beagle had to have three operations in his time because he kept eating tennis balls. One idiotic cat had a penchant for eating hair bobbles that would twist up and cause a blockage. A usually very energetic spaniel swallowed a whole potato, another a whole pack of 100 cotton buds and another ate a used tampon.

Another naughty terrier ate a very large walking sock, vomited a few times and stopped eating but didn't show us any sign of pain and nothing on x-ray. Only due to us knowing that the dog was usually very bouncy and crazy did we decide to open him up and found said sock but by this point, his guts were starting to turn black so we had to remove a portion of gut too. Although some material likes to remain elusive, sometimes things can be very obvious on an x-ray - none of us will ever forget the golden retriever who was known for going on walks with his owner on the golf course; he vomited up a couple of golf balls and was suddenly starting to look very unwell. An x-ray showed, very clearly, NINE golf balls in his stomach. Then there was a Labrador who ate several stones per week from the owner's brand new gravel drive that the owner had to decide to pave back over. Again, very easy to spot that one on an x-ray; the challenging part is working out whether they are small enough to be making their way through the guts or not! The owner had the expense of the vet bill, followed by the even greater expense of re-paving

one spot by the fence and every time a car came along, she would chase it the length of the fence and then return to her original position, repeating the process all day long. Inside, she'd stare at the lightbulb above the kitchen table for half an hour at a time. We think OCD behaviours are linked to stress but Tess had a very good amount of exercise and interaction from all of us. She was a rescue though and we don't know what happened previously.

These odd behaviours have caused one of our vets at our practice to become particularly confused due to the fact that English wasn't her first language. She was being taught various idioms and phrases by us all so when an owner came in and told her the dog was licking the back door, she thought she was being very clever by knowing that this was a slang term for its *bottom*. She did a thorough rectal examination, finding nothing and the owner looking on aghast. Turns out, the dog was licking the actual back door of the house! Let's hope no animal comes in to see her because it is licking the front door..

So we do love any stories of animals doing silly things. We still reminisce about some of these stories at lunch breaks or get togethers. If your pet does something particularly strange or funny, please tell your vet when you see them, it puts a smile on our face!

HOUSE VISITS

There are occasions in my line of work where we have to go to a pet's home to see them. Sadly, the most common reason for this is for a PTS, but we do also go to see ill animals or pets that are due their boosters if the owner cannot drive. In case you didn't know, 'put to sleep 'or PTS is the term we use a lot instead of 'euthanasia 'as a much more sensitive way of putting things. For house visits, if it is for a PTS, it is usually a much more pleasant experience for the cat or dog to be in their own environment, with their family around them. Therefore, even though the reason for our visit is a very sad one, we still like to go on these visits as it makes the situation as good as it can be for the pet and family. They do tend to be reasonably expensive as instead of taking up 15 minutes of a vet's time, you are using a nurse and a vet for anywhere between 45-90 minutes. Regardless of the reason for the house visit, they can be some of our favourite things to do. The bond you build with a family within their own home for a PTS means that we feel very privileged to be there. We can sometimes get the occasional cup of tea and biscuit too. Some of our oddest or most amusing stories come out of house visits; often providing comic relief in the saddest of times.

Firstly, there are some very strange houses with odd decoration choices that we see on house visits. For example, I have been to see a poorly dog in a house with a very strange audience - two cabinets full of Disney figurines. My colleague has been to a house full of porcelain dolls; particularly creepy given the house visit was at night. I went to see a dog for severe back pain a few years ago and the owner showed me through the house, going along a pathway he'd created between what must have been years and years of newspapers and magazines stacked up in the rooms. Why?!

We had a regular house visit that we used to go on every couple of weeks to a cat that had kidney disease and kept getting constipated. The lady used to leave the last few days of faeces in the litter tray for us to see and would, with her bare hands, pick them up and thrust them at us. She kept her little fingernail longer than all the rest and I swear it was just so that she could break up the faeces with it to show us the consistency. She was a very eccentric lady who kept us entertained with all the latest goings on in her family and complained loudly about her husband. The eccentricity clearly prevented her from cleaning the house much and along with the handling of cat faeces, we would always decline a cup of tea from this house! One of the strangest situations that I have been in is when doing a house visit PTS one evening in a house decorated with crystals, lit by candles and incense burning. When we perform a PTS, we have to place an intravenous catheter in the pet in order to be able to inject an overdose of an anaesthetic drug. In this particular house, the placement of the IV catheter was somewhat tricky due to only source of light being the candles. We managed to place it anyway and the owner then asked if we could take some of the dog's blood for her to keep. I'm still not sure exactly what she wanted to do with the blood as I didn't dare ask but I couldn't think of any regulations that meant that she couldn't have it. We often have requests for hair clippings or paw prints, but blood was something we hadn't experienced before!

There are also the houses that we go to visit that are just not conducive to a smooth exit with a beloved pet once it has passed away. Usually, once we have performed a PTS, the owner will decide what they would like to happen to the body. Some people will want to bury the pet in the garden in their favourite place. One of my friends was once asked if she could check the size of the hole before she went through with the PTS! If they do not want to bury their pet, they will make the decision to cremate the body, sometimes choosing to have those ashes back in a casket. If the body is to be cremated, we have to gently remove the body from the house in the most dignified way that we can and take it back to the practice. With cats and small dogs, one of us will carry them out of the house, wrapped in a blanket. However, if a dog weighs more than about 10kg, we often gently move them onto a stretcher and cover them over with a blanket. There have been quite a few times where this stretcher has been just too long or wide to fit around certain doorways or corridors and we have to gently tilt the stretcher to get it to fit. One house that we visited was on a very steep slope with a staircase leading down from the front door to the road, where the pet ambulance was parked. This meant that the stretcher was on about a 45 degree slope, with the 35kg body on it. As you can guess, the poor boy started to slide down the stretcher; only with my nurse's very quick raising of her end and a sudden squatting at my end, did we stop the inevitable happening. Luckily, the owner saw the funny side and commented that the dog had tripped down the stairs a few times in his life so it would have been fitting in some ways.

There was one time when I was on a house visit to put to sleep one of my client's dogs, and the whole family was clustered around the dog that we were saying goodbye to. I had been looking after this dog for a few weeks and he was a lovely boy and his family were very nice people too, so I was feeling a bit emotional myself. Once the injection had taken effect and the moment had come for myself and the nurse to depart, I suggested that their other dog was let into the room so that she could see what had happened to Hector. She came bounding in, saw that her family were upset and rushed to their side in turn to give them some love. She then spotted Hector in his bed on the sofa, looked at him and immediately started trying to dig a hole in sofa next to him. The mother of the family started laughing and soon everyone else joined in too. The nurse and I looked at each other in a very confused way; the mother then says,

"She never did like him much! She's clearly trying to bury him!"

Turns out Hector had been a bit of a bully to her given he was top dog in the house, and she may now have been looking forward to getting some of the attention from her owners. Animals giving you comic relief when you need it most!

There are also the houses that we like to go to visit just because they are very nice houses! You get a lot of great ideas for locations of your own house by visiting random dead end roads that you would never normally visit, or decor ideas from someone who can afford to pay an interior designer and has the most exquisite home. Then there are the houses that are so amazing that we know full well we could never afford ourselves so it is a glimpse into another world. There was an occasion when I was sent to vaccinate a group of 4 cats for an elderly lady who couldn't get the cats into the vets easily. The house was so lovely and the nurse and I got to see every inch of it by chasing the cats around the rooms in order to examine and vaccinate them! Clearly, they knew we were veterinary staff, just from our green tops and smell - not an uncommon problem; several of my friends have had to find cats under reclining chairs and in wardrobes. One of my colleagues has been to one particularly spectacular house a couple of times - one of the most expensive houses in the country, so I'm told. There are staff that are employed just to look after the animals and the cats have their own wing of the house!

Obviously, for my friends who work in farm animal or equine practice, it is a much more common occurrence to go to the farm or stables than it is for us that work in small animal practice.

I know that a few of them get a full cooked lunch or breakfast from some of the farmers, though this probably only goes part way to making up for being out in the freezing cold of winter, examining cows. I can concur from my days of work experience that the warmest place to be on those days is with your hand up a cow's backside! Sometimes, these vets will also get asked about the farm dog or cat whilst out. One of my friends once gave the farmer some kaolin paste to help improve his dog's diarrhoea and told him to give 5ml per day. When she returned a couple of weeks later to recheck the cows, she asked how the dog was doing. The farmer remarked that he was much better but that the paste had been so tricky to administer - he'd had to find the thickest needle he could. Turns out, instead of putting the paste into the food, he'd been injecting it into the scruff of the neck! The poor dog didn't seem to have any lasting effects though and given some cow drugs are given as injections by the farmer, we could see where the confusion came from.

Unfortunately, there are some times when a house visit is not possible due to us being fully booked, or it is not in the animal's best interest - such as in an emergency. In these situations we would strongly recommend getting a taxi into us, it is much cheaper and there are a few services out there that will bring animals. In fact, one of my friends works at a referral hospital and a couple of times a year needs a bag of blood from a cat with a particular blood group for a transfusion. There is a regular donor that lives about 45 minutes away that gets put into a taxi, in a cat basket, by her owner. The taxi then drives her to the referral hospital, the blood is taken for a transfusion, she is monitored for a couple of hours and gets sent back by the same taxi service! That cat will have saved many lives, and it is well behaved enough not to bother about all the travelling and stress of having blood taken.

So, when appropriate, house visits can be a very rewarding part of our jobs for a variety of reasons. We are always happy to make life that bit easier for people and especially for a PTS. They also get us out of the mania of the practice for an hour or so!

HITTING THE VEIN THE FIRST TIME ROUND

There are many situations in veterinary medicine where we have to insert some kind of needle into the vein of an animal. For blood tests, the most commonly used vein is the jugular vein in the neck. For placing intravenous catheters (IV catheters), we tend to use the cephalic vein on the front legs, though blood tests can be taken from this vein too. We place IV catheters for a variety of reasons - when animals are coming in for anaesthetics, if we are putting them on a drip or if we are performing a PTS.

In order to be able to get the needle in the vein, there are a few hurdles we have to jump through first. To begin with, we must clip a patch of fur over the vein. The helps a lot with visibility of the vein but it is mainly due to sterility; we cannot possibly disinfect a patch of fur properly. With a blood test where the needle is placed in the vein and pulled back out again after a few seconds, we can get away without clipping it, but for an IV catheter to be placed, it is essential to clip the fur. This then allows us to sterilise the skin with chlorhexidine, surgical spirit or both. Both of these actions can cause pets to freak out. The noise of the clippers can be terrifying to some animals, especially those that hate the groomers. Most cats will never have experienced that noise before and can often try to immediately leap out of the nurse's arms when they hear the noise. Often, once they realise the clippers make noise but cause no pain, they do calm down. Even the act of putting spirit on the area of skin can cause some animals to flinch because it feels very cold. Sometimes it isn't the animal that is the problem with fur clipping, it is the owner telling us that they have a show next week and they really cannot have a clipped patch of fur. Our thoughts are thus: if it is a blood test then yes, we will try our best, though in a fluffy animal this can be very tricky and may mean that we have to place the needle in many times before we finally hit the vein. For an IV catheter, no. If your pet is in need of one of these, it is probably not well enough to attend that show and if you're bringing it in for an elective procedure, try delaying that until after the show. The alternative is that we put the IV catheter in and wait to see if your pet gets phlebitis (infection around the vein) and a swollen leg; that may also ruin the chances of winning the show.

So once we have achieved step one and two, we then go to step three - actually getting the needle into the vein. This is when any number of things can happen. About 75% of the time, the animals are very well behaved and will allow themselves to be held appropriately. This usually entails a nurse (or receptionist at a branch practice!) holding them in a certain way that reduces all our chances of being bitten, whilst at the same time being as kind as possible to the animal and placing pressure in particular places that make them feel as though they can't move, without hurting them. With their seventh hand, they then need to lift the head up to allow us to raise and see the jugular vein, or hold out a foreleg and raise the cephalic vein for us. For some animals, this requires a second nurse too to act as a 'bum stop 'as the instinctive reactions for a lot of animals is to try to wiggle backwards. With some animals, we don't ever get beyond this point as the physical act of being held is far too stressful if they're not used to being handled such as very young puppies or kittens. In elderly patients, this can also be due to discomfort as they are arthritic and sore. If the pet does cooperate with being held, then a lot of the time they will be fine for the insertion of the needle too. Some animals may flinch ever so slightly, something we are always prepared for. If the pet is healthy, a normal weight, with normal length legs and conformation, then 90% of the time, in a well behaved animal, we can hit the vein first time round. This will still makes us do a little internal jig, no matter how old we are and how many thousands of times we have done it.

For some reason, even when everything works in your favour, sometimes the vein just remains elusive. Either it doesn't raise properly and appear in the right place, or it is very 'bouncy '- where it seems to just jump away from the needle when inserting it. It may take a few attempts or a fresh pair of eyes but eventually we will get there in these situations. However, a reasonable portion of the time, animals will not just sit there and accept a needle entering their body. We can very much understand this as they have no clue as to why we are doing it and as much as anyone says needles don't hurt, we all know that they aren't pleasant either. The reactions to needles can be very extreme though. Some animals will try to 'kebab 'themselves. This is when we are trying to take blood from the neck, and as soon as the needle hits the skin, the animal slams its head down onto the needle. With a firmer grip holding the head back, we can sometimes overcome this movement. It is a reasonably dangerous way for the animal to act though - there are many other vital structures in the neck! I have heard stories from clients of needles causing a laceration to the jugular vein and the pet bleeding profusely. I have never seen or heard of this from any vets or vet nurses though so I'm not sure if these stories are internet scaremongering or not! Regardless, if any animal tries to kebab itself more than once, we try to take blood from the leg instead. The problem with this is that it is a much smaller vein and in cats and small dogs, it can take up to a minute to get the blood out of the leg - that is a long time for an animal to stay still for!

Another reaction to insertion of a needle is to try to wiggle and move in any way possible to stop it from happening. We can usually rope in another nurse or vet to help hold the pet, or firmly tap it on the top of its head repeatedly, to distract it from the needle. The danger comes when the animal starts to try to use its teeth or claws to stop us. This often occurs in spoilt dogs or those that are super nervous. It can also occur with any cat because, well, it is a cat. For a dog, this can be reasonably easy to stop by placing a muzzle on them. Occasionally, this has the unforeseen benefit of calming them down too. For cats, it is much trickier! There are such things as cat muzzles, but they cover their whole face including their eyes. Again, this can actually calm them down but for some, it can freak them out even more. To stop them using their nails, we can make them into a kitty burrito by wrapping them up in a towel, with just their neck and head out or one of their front legs. With a lot of growling, meowing and sweating from the vet and nurses, we can then finally do what we need to do.

In about 5% of cases, no matter what we do, we cannot get the pet to cooperate and we have to resort to a sedation to get the blood test or place the IV catheter. Obviously this is commonly the case with wiggly, tiny puppies and kittens. We often also get owners who say that their adult pet will be much happier with them helping to hold them or being present in the room. Occasionally, this is the case - in situations where they have severe separation anxiety or are rescue dogs that have been mistreated in the past. Some of the time though, dogs are only acting in an anxious way because they are trying to protect their owners. I have lost count of the times when a dog is eyeing me up, wiggling away from me, crawling up the owner and growling at me when I try to examine it with the owner holding it then when we take it to the nurses to hold, they are entirely different dogs; far less nervous, even sometimes wagging their tails and wanting a cuddle from us. It is the fear of us going near to and hurting their owner that is making them behave in such a way, so always do let us try to do these things with the dog away from you. If they are worse away from you, trust me it is in our best interests to bring them straight back to you. I once had to take a blood test from a dog that was sat up on its owner's shoulder, as this was the only place it would let us do it!

As well as badly behaved animals, we also have another difficulty to contend with - animals that are too fat or have malformed legs. If a pet is overweight, there is a layer of fat between the skin and the vein which means that we cannot see where the vein is 'raising'. With experience, we know where the vein should be and we can make a good guess as to where to put the needle but if there is any deviation from the standard con-formation, we will struggle and likely have to insert many nee-dles before we find the vein - another reason to keep your pets at a normal weight! Even in skinny animals, some breeds have very short legs or those that are twisted or malformed, making it much harder to place IV catheters. The worse breeds for this are the Dachshund and Basset Hound though bulldogs and pugs aren't too far behind. For the brachycephalic breeds, we also have to make sure we don't hold them in a way that restricts their breathing or causes them too much stress as they can pass out. If we get a vein first time in any of these breeds, its not an internal jig that we perform, but usually a real one, leading to a few pats on the back!

There is one situation above all others that you want to get the IV catheter in first time round - during euthanasias. We do everything we can to make the process as smooth as we can for the family and getting an IV catheter in first time can cer-tainly add to that. Unfortunately, a lot of elderly animals have collapsed or fragile veins that can easily blow. When poorly and dehydrated, these veins are much smaller and the blood pressure can be very low which makes things even harder. There is a lot of pressure on us in this situation and we really are trying our best. We will often suggest placing the IV catheter out the back, with the nurses holding the pet. This is because, as with most things in life, when you are under pressure from owners watching you are less likely to hit the vein first time. If placing it is stressful for your pet, we will often suggest that we give them a sedation first so that they are then asleep for the placement, unaware of the needles.

We have rare occasions when we need to take blood from an exotic animal or place an IV catheter in a rabbit for an anaesthetic or a drip. For rabbits, we use the vein that runs down the side of their ear. They virtually all need some form of sedation, or feel very poorly, to allow us to place the catheter. The size of the IV catheter rivals those placed in babies and can be very satisfying to place. I've seen my incredible colleague take tiny amounts of blood from rats, parrots, tortoises and snakes. All of these need an anaesthetic to be able to take the blood which makes them immobile, but doesn't stop the tricky challenge of locating the vein under the scales and feathers.

No matter how long you have been a vet or nurse for, you will always have that happy feeling when the needle goes in the vein first time. Every practice will have a 'queen 'or 'king 'of the vein who will often be called upon to get the blood if all else fails - usually your most senior nurse. Even they will still be very chuffed with themselves if they get the vein on a wiggly, dehydrated, dachshund puppy though.

HAVING A LAUGH
WITH COLLEAGUES

We have to spend a large proportion of our day being sensible and mature; having serious conversations with owners, working out plans for inpatients, concentrating on performing complex surgeries and more besides. It is therefore a relief when you have some time for a lunch break or a quick cup of tea and you can relax for a bit. It is in these times that we can, very quickly, realise that we are having ridiculous, immature conversations with our colleagues and laughing a lot at something only a seven year old would normally find amusing. Given the nature of our job, these conversations often involve the latest silly thing that an animal has done, or some kind of animal excrement.

There are so many stories that have been had about poo. There was the time a nurse was holding a small dog up under one arm, did what she needed to do, put the dog back in the kennel and then reached into her pocket. There she found a perfectly formed little poo that the dog had clearly just deposited into her pocket, on her phone and pens. On more than one occasion, a vet or nurse has had to change their top, trousers or their whole outfit due to a pet urinating or having profuse diarrhoea all over them. Similar situations occur with anal glands; I have lost count of the number of times that animals have needed these scent glands expressing but they had been blocked and you had to apply quite a bit of pressure. This then results in the glands suddenly shooting across the room and up the walls, if you're lucky. There have certainly also been many occasions where the anal gland secretion has ended up the back of a colleague, on the owner's arms or, most pleasant of all - on our faces or in our hair. The only good thing about this situation is the way that you can make your colleagues laugh.

One of my favourite stories comes from one of the other vets who was examining a chinchilla. It had something called paraphimosis - where the penis gets engorged and become stuck out of the sheath. This happens reasonably often in puppies that are going through puberty but the condition in a chinchilla is something we hadn't seen before. The funniest thing about a chinchilla penis is how long and thin it is. The treatment for the condition is to use a lot of lube and try to replace the penis back into the sheath and keep it there. My colleague managed this with the chinchilla - but only after it had ejaculated all over her arm. Obviously, many jokes were then made about this situation for weeks after. If simple manipulation doesn't allow you to get the penis back in (whatever the species!), then you need to reduce the swelling by simple osmosis - holding the penis in a cup of sugar until the water has all leaked out and the penis is back to a more normal size. Again, whenever this happens, whichever vet is performing the act gets many comments thrown their way for the next few days. You'd think that we would find this all very mundane after a while, but no, we are all incredibly immature at heart.

A similar condition can happen in bitches when they are in season and they can get a vaginal prolapse where the inside of their vagina hangs out of the external opening. I had a lovely rescue dog come to see us that this had happened to; she didn't have a name at the time and quickly got branded 'vagina dog' after the second time that I had to replace it with a good deal of sugar, lubrication and my fingers. The fun doesn't stop there either. Our maturity levels do extend to our bosses too. Both of my male bosses were bald and we would quite often make jokes about what we could use as a toupé for them. My favourite was when I had to remove a dog's scrotum, along with his testicles, because he had testicular cancer in his old age. It hadn't spread and we knew that surgery would be curative. The scrotum ended up being a lovely circle of wrinkly, hairy skin that looked perfect on top of the bosses head. My other boss is particularly good at performing anal gland removal surgery and has been labelled 'Butt-man 'instead of Batman.

Due to the fact that we spend a lot of our days discussing silly situations with animals, we are certainly not shy about discussing our own bodily functions too. Most of us have been infected with some kind of animal bacteria or parasite during our time in training or at work. I have had a parasite called giardia, a single-celled organism that burrows into the intestine of the dog, cat or human and causes vomiting, diarrhoea, anorexia and weight loss. I was unlucky enough to acquire this parasite whilst at a charity in India with some of my friends neutering animals, treating wounds and illnesses and giving rabies vaccinations. I can pinpoint the moment the infection probably happened - when a dog wagged its tail into the gutter of poo and then flicked the poo into my mouth! My colleagues have had campylobacter, a bacteria that causes food poisoning in humans but chronic diarrhoea in pet animals, and cryptosporidium, another parasite like giardia that most commonly occurs in sheep. It is not too surprising therefore that a high number of vets and vet nurses suffer from irritable bowel syndrome as a consequence of gut scarring. It is commonplace to discuss ways to help with this and how some of us are doing at the time. It means that a lot of us have very amusing stories to tell about the last time we didn't quite make it to the toilet in time..

If you know a vet or a nurse, you will know that we can discuss anything at any time - including when eating. This is a constant source of annoyance amongst some of my friends who aren't medical but we genuinely just forget that some people are more sensitive about these things. To us, it is very normal to sit around the lunch table and discuss pus and blood. We also like to play the game of 'how much would you have to be paid to eat this? 'This usually involves pus, diarrhoea, testicles, organs, blood clots and such like.

Our maturity levels don't reach their height there. We can also get the giggles over immature words. We have some elderly clients that don't quite know that there is a double meaning to the word 'pussy 'and will be stroking their cats whilst having their vaccinations, saying what a good little pussy they are. Sometimes there are consults booked in for us by reception, saying 'pussy wound'; for future reference, the word you are looking for is 'purulent 'when talking about pus.

Then there are the pet's names. Our all time favourite has to be a little old lady called Mrs Bushe who quite innocently called her cat 'Messi'. Yes, Messi Bushe. There are some very imaginative names that make us giggle too but we are also very impressed. Recently, I've seen two Greek rescue cats, named after the heroes of the Trojan War, Agamemnon and Menelaus. Rather tenuously but fabulously, these cats are called Agamemcat and Meowlaus. We do love an imaginative name; one of my friends has called their dog Goose which is something I haven't seen before. We used to see a lot of Ceefers and Deefers - as in 'c' for cat or 'd' for dog (yeah, seriously) but lots of people cottoned on to this and it became less original. Some owners have been determined to call their next male pet a certain name, only to find out that they are actually female so we have a few female pets called male names, my favourite being 'Dave 'the female cocker spaniel. Then there are those that we really don't want to have to say out loud in the waiting room, such as 'Madame Queenie Von Floofington' and 'Princess Tinkerbell'. Oh and a word of warning - naming your cats as a pair like 'salt and pepper' will doom one of them to an early death. If you believe in such things. I don't, but a lot of the veterinary profession is very superstitious; certainly don't say that a particular day is looking 'quiet' as it will be your fault when all the emergencies turn up.

We often like a good singalong to the radio if the day is not too crazy busy. Once animals have had their pre-medication for their anaesthetic, they are very sleepy and cuddly and thus very amenable to being held in our arms and having a little dance when brought through to have their surgery. We sometimes wiggle their arms in time to the music too, like they're dancing. There is something slightly strange about doing a routine surgery and cutting testicles off a dog whilst singing along to Britney or Beyoncé. Not quite as morbid as the time I was at a slaughterhouse and the workers were singing along to 'Walking on Sunshine 'whilst removing the organs and skin from the dead animals. Though I guess in both these instances, the things we do become so routine in our days that we become immune to the oddity of the situation. Given we have many serious and sad moments in our days, it is a way for us to cope and find some relief from being upset and sensible.

As a group of people that spend all our time together at work, we very quickly become close and can discuss most things in life from sex and relationships to the latest political or socio-economic views. We now know that some of the men place talcum powder on their testicles every day, how often and what time of day we all change our underwear, the ups and downs of each person's relationships or dating stories and all our 'out-there 'views on the world. We know that it is a safe space where any of us can say anything that we want and that we accept all views. Although many of these things cause a lot of laughs, we generally don't judge and love the fact that our middle-aged male bosses will join in with the same conversations as the eighteen year old, female nurses.

One of the most hilarious topics is all the things the staff's children get up to. We have all met these children as they will come in to the practice at various points to meet us or if their mum or dad needs to pick something up on a day off. A few of them will actively ask to come into the practice whenever their parents have a day off because they love to see some of the animals in the kennels, come to chat to us all and steal biscuits from the table. The head nurse's six year old son was my 'boyfriend 'for the first few years of my career; at least I was guaranteed a home made Valentine's card! She often brought this very chatty son in to see us, along with her younger daughter who has a fantastic resting bitch-face. The boss's middle son really did have a sadistic streak; he once defaecated on his bedroom floor in protest of something he didn't want to do and when asked to write a list of things he wanted to do in his summer holidays, 'destroy the world 'and 'eat ice cream 'were on about the same level.

It is one of the best parts of our jobs to have colleagues that we become so close to and can have such a laugh with. These colleagues are there for us to dry our tears when having a particularly stressful or sad day and they usually recount one of the many stories that have been a source of amusement previously. You have to be able to laugh at odd things in our profession because if you didn't, or if you spent the whole time dwelling on the upsetting times, you'd spend a lot of time crying instead. I know a lot of my non-vet friends think some of the things we do and say are incredibly immature or strange, but we have to in order to get by some days. Plus, it's much more fun to be childish sometimes.

A DAY WHERE
NOBODY CRIES

In contrast to the previous chapter about the times we get to laugh and enjoy aspects of the job, there are sadly many situations in which people around us, and vets themselves, become very upset. The next two chapters are a bit gloomy but they have a very strong message behind them: why there is a much larger proportion of veterinary professionals that turn to suicide when compared to other jobs.

The most obvious place to start when talking about 'people crying within a vet practice 'are the owners of pets. If an animal is particularly poorly, or if the owners are particularly worried, then we are likely to get some very upset people in our consult room. Of course, if the pet is here to be PTS, then it goes without saying that most people in the room will be in tears. In any of these situations, you have to deal with your own emotions about the issue as well as the owner's. I have heard many heartbreaking stories in these moments that have made me want to cry too. One of the worst situations is always when the pet in question is the last living thing that someone associates with a lost loved one. We have many elderly clients who have pets that become ill and they are just not ready to let go of them due to them being their lost wife or husband's pet. They know the right thing to do in this situation is to end the pet's suffering but seeing the

grief appear again for their lost partner, as well as for the pet itself, is horrible to witness. When the pet is unwell and we need
to perform diagnostics and keep it in the hospital, we feel extra
pressure in these situations to get the animal better as quickly as
possible. If we find something that is not treatable, or if the pet
doesn't respond to treatment, it is one of the worst phone calls
that we have to make as you know the pet means more to them
than most.

The same can be said for those people who are sadly not able
to have children, and the pets have all the extra love put upon
them and things are even more difficult when they are ill. There
are a few memories that spring to mind that were particularly
heartbreaking. We had a very unwell, young beagle in to see
us who had terrible gut issues and despite everything we did,
we couldn't seem to improve his appetite and weight loss. The
owners came to visit and were in tears, desperate for us to help
him because they had bought him for their son who had been
diagnosed with cancer. They thought having a dog to get up for
and go for walks with would help motivate him through his
treatment. If he died, they thought the son would be so devastated that it would set him back in his own treatment. Luckily
that night, my colleague was researching online and calling specialists for any ideas as to what more we could do and came
across a very rare disease that can affect beagles, with a simple
treatment of vitamin B injections. He made a miraculous recovery and went back home to his family a couple of days later.

Then there was Mango, the Labrador that a husband had bought
for his young wife when he knew he was dying and wanted her
to have something new and fun in her life to focus on. She was
named after his favourite food and was unfortunately a disaster
of a dog. She got glaucoma in one eye and had to have it removed
as it didn't respond to treatment. She ruptured her cruciate liga-
ments in each knee and had to have operations to fix them both.
Every time the owner had to leave her with us, she would be

so upset, thinking about her husband as well as the dog. Due to the world being very unfair, Mango got another terrible illness reasonably young in life and had to be put to sleep far too soon. We cannot imagine what the owner was going through in this scenario but I don't think there was a dry eye in the building that day.

We also all had a soft spot for a lovely elderly couple who owned a Rottweiler that we loved seeing and Mr Early would always bring him in to get him weighed and have a chat with the receptionists, or come in for a consult with a nurse or a vet about any issues Max may have been having. Then one day, Mr Early came in with Max, very upset and told us that his wife had sadly been taken ill herself, and over the following weeks we got regular updates until the time when she passed away. Max was starting to become unwell himself and was limping on one of his forelegs, which didn't resolve with painkillers. Knowing that any Rottie over the age of 6 that starts limping could well have a bone tumour, we really didn't want to take X-rays of his leg but knew we must. The sinking feeling we had when we saw those X-rays and the obvious pattern of a bone tumour...life can be very cruel. After a few weeks of strong painkillers, Max could not cope anymore and poor Mr Early had to lose his wife and his beloved dog in the space of a couple of months.

Sadly, these stories are not the only examples we have of particularly devastating moments. Any day when we do not have to console a crying owner with the offer of a tissue, a squeeze to the hand or a hug, is a day that we like.

Unfortunately, a lot of the time, our staff are reduced to tears too in these moments. A reasonable proportion of the time, this is because we are also grieving the loss of an animal we have treated for a long time. Vets, nurses and receptionists will all become very attached to pets and it is only natural for us to be upset by their departure. One of us will often be found with a colleague crying into our shoulders, wrapped up in a hug and being sent upstairs to get a glass of water. All of us can only afford to be upset for a matter of moments, before having to dry off our tears and go onto the next consult or face the next customer in reception. Our practice manager watched a programme about vets on the television once and we happened to have a meeting the next day. She wanted to pass on her feelings about how she thought it must be such a hard thing to do, to be upset and consoling owners one minute, then the next having to pull ourselves together and be happy and jolly to the next clients who bring in their new puppy. It is something that all of us have had to learn to deal with and we have to have the ability to compartmentalise our emotions and not always show how we are truly feeling.

However, there are a few times in my career that I can still remember as being particularly low points and the ability to build up a wall and not become too emotional was far too difficult. The first was after I had been in practice for about 18 months and I was on call for the whole weekend. At this point, we did our own out of hours service overnight so we were working non-stop for 48 hours. During these 48 hours, a total of twelve animals died. A few of them were elderly animals that were brought in for pre-planned euthanasias. It was a hot weekend in the summer and sadly, two of them were British bulldogs that had dropped down dead due to their inability to breathe properly and were brought in for cremation. There was another sudden death at home that we had to perform a post-mortem on. Then the other few were animals that had been ill for hours to days, and had conditions that we couldn't fix and they either passed away by themselves or we had to put them to sleep. The final straw for me was when a Great Dane with a twisted stomach came in on the Sunday evening. His stomach had been twisted and bloated for several hours and when we operated, his stomach was purple and his blood pressure was very low. The surgery to untwist the stomach, relieve the bloating and attach the stomach to the abdominal wall to prevent recurrence took over two hours and was very difficult given the size of the 90kg dog. Afterwards, his heart couldn't cope with the stress that had been placed upon his body and he had a terrible arrhythmia. Despite many painkillers and drugs for the heart, he died overnight. I had a day off the next day - most of which I spent crying for all the animals I couldn't save that weekend.

The saddest days are always when you lose young animals. A few years ago, we had a nine week old corgi puppy come in out of hours one Sunday morning. He was retching and seemed bloated, with an extremely painful abdomen. He would cry as soon as you put any pressure on his abdomen and this didn't resolve with very strong painkillers. An X-ray was very inconclusive as young animals have different density of fat that makes things very difficult to interpret. We had to open him up under anaesthetic and work out what was making him so painful. Astonishingly, his stomach had twisted - something that usually only happens in the aforementioned large dogs. He had something called septic peritonitis which is when there is infected fluid in the abdominal cavity that shouldn't be there, due to the twisted stomach. Septic peritonitis is known to be very painful. We did all we could and he astonishingly survived the anaesthetic. As soon as he woke up, despite the morphine type pain killer that he was on, he started whimpering in pain. The nurse and I looked at each other, wondering what we could do, hoping that more painkillers and time would make him better. He then crashed and died in front of us; we performed CPR and brought him back to life twice. At this point, I called the owner and explained that if he crashed again, given the level of pain he was in, it wasn't fair to carry on with CPR. They agreed and he shortly passed away. We had spent six hours trying to save him and it wasn't enough. The nurse and I cried as we cleared up everything we had used and went home, hoping not to be called in again for the rest of the day. I had previously arranged to see one of the other nurses on my way home as long as it wasn't too late in the day. I rang her doorbell and her mother answered the door and I burst into tears again, as her daughter came running out to hug me. To this day, her mother still tells everybody she knows just how much vets care about their patients as she can remember how I was that day.

In my career, I have had to PTS many animals way before their time. A two year old Labrador with aggressive lymphoma; a Chihuahua with a congenital liver problem; a three year old Golden Retriever with likely stomach cancer; two cats under the age of a year who had FIP plus several cats and dogs who have been hit by cars, buses or trains when they have barely begun their lives. Most recently, we had a seven week old poodle puppy that was brought in by the breeder as it was vomiting, not eating and seemed painful. The pressure was on, as this puppy was destined for the breeder's friend who was suffering with PTSD and she thought a dog may help. The puppy had a large umbilical hernia and it transpired that his pancreas had herniated, along with some of his guts. We performed surgery to repair the hernia and hoped that with intensive medical care, he would get better. The nurse and I spent a whole Sunday caring for him and he seemed to recover reasonably well overnight with the nurse having him with her in the bedroom. Unfortunately, it was not meant to be and my colleague had to put him to sleep the next day as he took a turn for the worse and become more painful again. The breeder, the nurse and I were all devastated and again, spent time crying about how unfair life can be. All my vet colleagues have had similar thing happen in their career and it upsets every one of us, the male vets included. Seeing your male bosses cry over an animal is something that shows that no matter how long you have been in the profession and how tough you can be, the job can really get to you.

It is not only the death of the animals that can make veterinary staff cry. A lot of the time, it is because of the owners. Most of our clients are lovely and think that all our staff are wonderful. However, some people seem to think that vet nurses and receptionists are below them and are not worthy of their respect. There are many times that I have seen them reduced to tears because of the words of pet owners. The majority of the time, the thing they are shouting at them for is not their fault. They don't have any control over our pricing, when tests are reported, when there are spaces for animals to be booked in for appointments or when a person can be guaranteed a call back. Even if it is something that they can help with, since when did using abusive language and being confrontational get you anywhere in life? If people put in a complaint, we are far more likely to be respectful and help resolve the issues quickly if you treat all our staff with the same respect. If you are nasty, our inclination to help you is much less. It astonishes me that time after time, people resort to being horrible rather than talking things through in a calm and logical manner. As previously mentioned, some of the nurses, especially the trainees, get abused for not knowing what they are talking about even though they will know more than the average member of the public. The reception staff will be telling owners the correct information about needing a medication review appointment or about flea treatment and the owners will insist on speaking to a vet instead. As soon as a vet comes out to speak to these owners, they are suddenly nice as pie and think we deserve a more kind and respecting tone of voice. Well, you may think that we deserve your respect but once you've behaved like that, you most certainly do not have our respect any more. It is often noted on your file and if there are several incidents, then we have every right to ask you to find pet care elsewhere.

As vets, we get our fair share of abuse too. A lot of the time this is due to worry about their pet, we can understand it and people do actually apologise once their pet is better. Often, it is about the cost of the veterinary treatment (discussed previously!) or that something wasn't diagnosed quickly enough. We cannot talk to your pet; everything we do is us trying our best to find an answer to help your pet as quickly as possible and without putting them through a load of unnecessary tests. All vets will have a list of possible diagnoses in their minds that will include the most likely and common options, through to some more rare diseases. We could admit your pet and perform fifteen tests all in one day, spending a lot of your money and putting your pet through a lot of needles, X-rays, ultrasounds, anaesthetics and assessments. The other option is to trial some treatment for what we think it is first and then if that doesn't work, go on to do one or two tests and keep going with this until we find the answer. When you are at the start of this diagnostic journey, it can seem daunting and long or costly. We really are trying to help your pet, whilst at the same time not exhausting your bank balance or putting your pet through things that may be unnecessary.

If your pet is critically unwell, then obviously we can speed up the process as much as possible, often doing every test in the space of a few hours until we reach a diagnosis and save their life. We know you are worried, but shouting at us or our staff will not mean that we can get a diagnosis any quicker. Also, the individual associate vets do not have any control over the pricing of the medication or tests. In independent practices, it is the partners that will set pricing in line with what other vets in the area are charging so that nothing is unfairly priced. My bosses would have meetings every six months or so to evaluate our costings compared to other vets in the vicinity and we would often be slightly cheaper and this is why we would get all the charities bringing animals to us. Yet we would still get comments from clients on a regular basis about how much we charge. It really does start to wear you over time, especially on a day that was filled with stress and sadness.

In corporate practices, the vets working have even less control over the pricing. If you are angry in any of these situations, I would advise writing a polite but firm email to the practice manager rather than abusing staff who cannot change anything about it. Again, we are just trying to help your pet whilst sticking to legal requirements and trying to run a business so we can all continue to be here for your animals. One of my colleagues has had a man square up to him and threaten to punch him because he wouldn't allow him in the X-ray room. Another one of my vet colleagues sadly diagnosed a dog with an enlarged prostate that could be cancerous or benign. The owner had no money or insurance and was therefore told that we would just give anti-inflammatory painkillers so we knew he wouldn't be suffering. We offered the possibility of running a urine sample as the cheapest test, to see if we could diagnose any cancerous cells in the urine, just so he had some idea. When turning around to go to ring the practice manager to see if she was allowed to run the sample for free rather than charge the owner, the owner yelled that he didn't have the money for any of this. He said that he hoped 'they privatised the NHS, the vet became ill, couldn't afford treatment and he hoped she f****** died'. My colleague politely told him that she wouldn't be spoken to like that and asked the practice manager to call him later on that day. He promptly called the manager a c*** and was thus asked not to return to our practice.

I cannot think of a single one of my veterinary colleagues or vet friends who hasn't been reduced to tears in some way or another, regardless of their gender and personality. Next time you feel like taking out your anger out on any veterinary staff, please think about what may have been going on behind the scenes already that day. If you are worried or upset about your pet's care, please do write your concerns down in an email; I am absolutely not saying that you cannot have your say and express your opinions, but just in a calm and considered manner. You do not know what terrible things the staff have already had to deal with that day, or even what is going on in their personal lives that may mean they are only just holding things together anyway. Sadly, your words could be the final straw for some people.

A FULL NIGHT
OF SLEEP

There are many reasons why we may not get a full night of sleep in the veterinary world. The most obvious of these is 'out of hours' (OOH) work. When I first started work, my practice performed their own out of hours service all through the night for the first three years that I worked there. Nowadays, a lot of practices will turn over their phones to one of the aforementioned OOH providers at the end of the working day, around 7pm and take back control of the phone when they open. Some (like mine!) keep hold of the phone lines until about 10pm as this is when the majority of calls are made. I would estimate from personal experience that 80% of practices hand over to OOH providers now for some or all of the night. After three years of me being there, my practice was struggling to recruit new vets and several vets had left because of the stress of full, overnight OOH. If you manage to get a reasonable night of sleep then it is manageable, but if not, then you suffer for it the next day when you have to work a whole day shift too. Given the amount of mental health issues in the profession, a lot of vets are choosing to make their life that bit easier by choosing not to work at practices that do their own OOH.

It can have an impact on the animals too; I can remember a couple of times that by the end of the next working day, I could barely take in what an owner was telling me because of the fact that I only got a couple of hours of sleep the night before. Obviously, this is not safe and can, in extreme circumstances, mean that diagnoses are missed and can endanger the lives of the pets. When my practice couldn't hire any vets to replace those that had been lost, we made the difficult decision, as a team, to reduce our OOH commitments. We wanted this to impact our clients as little as possible so the nursing team decided that they would have a rota in place to sleep in the flat above the practice and come to check on the inpatients if needed and call the vet at home if worried. Obviously, this was compensated for with a small bonus for each night the nurse spent in the flat. This meant that we could retain the majority of our inpatients and not have to send them to the OOH provider. If we had any critical inpatients that needed more than one or two checks in the night then we would send them for optimum care at the OOH provider; this probably only happens about 5% of the time. Given that before this time both vet and nurse would have been staying up with these inpatients ourselves all night, before working the full shift the next day, this seemed a much safer option. If the nurses have a particularly bad night then we will try to send them home at lunchtime. Suddenly, we had a lot more applicants for our vacant vet slots too!

Now that it has been many years since I did overnight 'on call', I can look back on some of the stories and laugh. I can tell you that there are fewer better feelings than waking up to your normal alarm after a night of being on call, rather than in the middle of the night to the ringing of a phone! About 10% of our total OOH calls happened overnight but this probably meant you'd be woken up 1 in every 3 shifts. For the first few months of 'on call', you tend to sleep quite lightly as you are so conscious of the phone ringing. This means that you can answer the phone quite swiftly and have a reasonably 'awake' voice when you talk to the client. As time goes on, you become less terrified that you will sleep through the calls and you tend to get a few hours of deeper sleep. I can remember being awoken from deep sleep a few times and answering the phone with a garbled message that made no sense. The client would then be slightly confused and after a few seconds I'd repeat the message again, slightly more awake. Most clients don't realise that we are fast asleep and at home in bed when they call. Only once have I slept through a call - when I had a bad cold and had taken some medicine before bed. Luckily, the client ended up coming in the next morning to see me. I apologised profusely and the owner was very understanding; the dog hadn't been as unwell as she feared at the time and she said it had saved her the OOH fee!

One of my first overnight calls was for a dog that had vomited a couple of times. After establishing that the dog was well in itself and had eaten dinner that evening, I wasn't too worried and started to wonder if these were the type of people who would go into A&E if they had vomited a few times. We know it is difficult because animals cannot talk to you and tell you how they are feeling but if your dog is happy in itself and still keen to play, you can be assured that you don't have to wake anyone up! After the adrenaline of a phone call, most of us find that we lie awake for at least half an hour after hanging up so even if we don't have to see a case, it can still disturb our sleep to some extent, especially if you have more than one call in a night. There are many types of call that are more of a grey area as to whether they need to be seen. Owners want to be guided by you and although it is never the wrong thing to see a poorly animal, you don't want to spend the client's money or get them (or you!) out of bed unnecessarily. A dog that has had diarrhoea for 4 days, is now lethargic, not wanting to eat and has some blood in it's faeces - probably fine to wait the 6 hours until we open but they can take a down turn pretty quickly and would it be better to admit it for a drip at 2am? An elderly cat that hasn't eaten for 24 hours and has started vomiting - has it got a stomach upset or is it something more serious like a diabetic crisis; one is fine to wait until morning, the other isn't. You can ask certain questions to owners to guide you in your decision making and suggest whether animals are safe to wait until morning (and save the call out fee!) but sometimes we will lie there awake, wondering if we made the right decision and what happens if we are wrong and thus we lose an hour more of sleep anyway! We will always offer to see the pet in any of these situations so the ultimate decision lies with the owners but we know they are guided by us.

Having said that, there have been a few phone calls in the middle of the night that I have point blank refused to see. The first of these was somebody who called me to say that their cat had fleas. At 3am. Most definitely not a life-threatening emergency. Neither was the call about the dog with an ear infection. Or the lump they'd just found on their dog - I can assure you that even if it is sadly cancerous, twelve hours is not going to make any difference to the prognosis. Most of these scenarios beg the question - what are you doing examining your pet in the middle of the night? I suppose you can be forgiven if you do shift work and you think that we are just up all night, sitting in the practice waiting to be called but when the answerphone message says 'in the case of an *emergency*, please call... 'you'd think that people would think twice. I have had one lady call out of hours to make an appointment for her pet for the next day for a vaccination. Luckily this was in the evening so I wasn't asleep but I still don't have access to the computer system from my sitting room. My colleague actually did get out of bed at 5am to see a cat with fleas because the owner clearly earned so much money that paying for an emergency consult was more convenient for her. I'm not being facetious, she genuinely said that. Personally, I think my colleague was taking customer satisfaction to a whole new level there.

When we know that we are needed for a true emergency, even though we know it will give us less sleep, we are more than happy to spring out of bed, put our clothes on and drive into the practice. Examples of true emergencies that I have got out of bed for include: a dog that was retching without being sick, bloated and restless (a twisted stomach); a cat that had sudden onset paralysis to one or two back legs and was yowling (a blood clot lodged in a vessel); a seizure that lasted for more than four minutes and a couple of pets that had been hit by a car. This probably amounts to fewer times than I can count on my fingers but in these very serious situations, you are out of bed for many hours. Caesarian sections are another emergency that we see often at night as this is when the bitch will often decide to whelp! A lot of these emergencies past 10pm will now go to the brilliant OOH providers that at least get to go home and sleep the next day. The ones that call before 10pm still get to come to us. In this way, turning the phones over at 10pm still doesn't guarantee us a good night of sleep. There have been plenty of times that we have been called at 9.55pm for an emergency that then takes us a couple of hours to see. When we are back in bed, we are pumped full of adrenaline from the situation, especially if it was a true emergency.

A year ago, I was called to a very poorly 9 week old spaniel puppy who's brother had died a few days previously because he ripped up and ate a tea towel and didn't make it through the surgery at such a young age. This particular puppy had started to making strange little coughs and was a bit lethargic. He had eaten his dinner and had been fine earlier in the day so at first, I suggested that they leave him overnight and see how he was in the morning, thinking that maybe he had inhaled something or had a respiratory virus and the owners were hypersensitive due to the situation. After a couple of hours, about 9pm, they called back to say he was a bit worse and starting to whimper so they brought him in to see me. He was making these strange little sounds with every breath and when you palpated his abdomen, he would whimper and the noises would be more dramatic for a minute or two. We gave him a painkiller and took an X-ray and scanned his abdomen. The lungs looked reasonably clear except for one, small section that just looked odd. His abdomen also looked mainly normal but there was something not quite right that I just couldn't put my finger on.

As the hour went by, his signs were worsening and I was no closer to working out what was happening. Knowing it was something more unusual, I offered to refer him to a specialist. The owners were very worried that he may have eaten the same bit of tea towel and, though I couldn't find any evidence of this, the pressure was on to save this puppy. I sent him off to the referral centre, knowing I had done the best thing for the dog. I then lay awake, full of adrenaline and wondering if the owners thought I was a bad vet for not being able to find a diagnosis or if they were going to be angry that I had suggested he waited until the morning after the first call. All the possible scenarios went through my head, from the puppy dying and the owners suing me, to the referral vets saying that it was something simple and a GP vet could have fixed it. When you're just in your head at night, your powers of reasoning are thrown out of the window. There is no way any referral vet would ever bad mouth another vet, and I should have had more faith in my skills to know that if I couldn't find out what was wrong with the puppy, it was certainly not anything simple. I barely slept that night, went into the practice the next day and got an update from the referral centre. Their emergency vets didn't know what was wrong with it either but he was more settled on oxygen and with pain killers. Later that day, their specialist imaging vet worked out that there was a very small hole in the dog's diaphragm that was letting some of the abdominal contents into the chest - which explained all the signs and why things just didn't look right. The puppy had surgery and made a full recovery. It was likely a congenital defect and we wonder whether the other puppy had the same condition and that is why he didn't make it through his own surgery. The owners brought me a box of chocolates to their recheck appointment. Thus my many hours of worrying and not sleeping were all unnecessary!

If we see a pet earlier in the day and it is a tricky case and the animal is very poorly, we will still think about it when trying to get to sleep or our dreams will be plagued by scenarios involving the pet. I have lost track of the times that I have laid awake at the beginning of the night or awoken in the middle of the night after dreaming about a case. This is then built up in your mind to being even more than it is in the cold light of day. At that particular moment, you think of all the potential things you could have done wrong, the owner's money that you have spent, the fact that you could have left an animal suffering for longer than needed and that a 'better vet 'would have done things differently. If we cannot find an answer as to why your pet is ill, it really does bother us almost as much as it bothers you. There are even moments that I remember waking up in the early hours of the morning, suddenly remembering that I didn't call a client and that they must be angry. I have never known a vet to look at some results and think 'I promised that person I'd call them today but I don't think I can be bothered'. It will be because another pet came in that distracted us and then we genuinely forgot or, more likely, the results didn't come back on the day we expected them to or there was a mix up at the lab or with our system. The majority of the time, clients are fine with a call 12-24 hours after you said they would get it, and you have lost an hour of sleep for no reason.

Why does your subconscious decide to remind you of these things at such a random time? How can you go through an entire evening and not remember something and then when you're asleep, a little lightbulb goes off in your mind and 'ding 'you're awake? Then, yet again you start to think about how you've made the client angry or that the pet may have terrible blood results and you've left it without treatment for longer. I have even awoken in the night for far less important reasons that would be so easily resolved the next day; I didn't book that pet in for their appointment that they asked me to do whilst I was talking to them outside, away from the computer system; I forgot to write down the estimate of costs I gave a client so the next vet who sees the pet may unknowingly go over this estimate; I didn't take the blood pressure machine from one branch practice to another, ready for the appointment that morning; the list goes on. I imagine that not all vets have this inability to sleep properly due to the stresses of the job; I know a lot of people will sleep as soon as their head hits the pillow and not wake again until the morning. However, I also know that many of my colleagues and vet friends are very similar to me, and probably about once every two weeks will be kept up or being awoken in the night by worries of the job.

We are told that we are likely to be sued twice in our career as vets or vet nurses. Therefore, any one of these things that we lose sleep over are things that we worry will turn into one of these lawsuits. Luckily, we do have the Veterinary Defence Society (VDS) to protect us against a lot of claims. The majority of the time, owner complaints are rejected because the vet or nurse didn't actually do anything wrong. This is a common theme but even when you know you haven't done anything wrong, it still replays in your mind at night and causes you excess worry and sleep deprivation. Unfortunately, a lot of complaints made actually come down to money in the end. It sickens me that a lot of people are willing to complain about an individual, causing that individual a lot of needless worry, just to get some money off. My bosses hate to 'reward 'this behaviour with money off but it often makes the problem go away very quickly, causing far less stress and worry to the staff involved. If you truly thought that your pet's care was substandard, and that they had suffered as a result, then money shouldn't mean anything to you.

Sadly, everyone makes mistakes in life and we are no exception. Nobody can tell me that they are perfect and have never made any mistakes. We certainly do misdiagnose things occasionally but it is not our intention and we will have thought that was the best course of action at the time. Trust me, we think about these mistakes far more than you would think and it plagues our mind for years. I have two situations that I still think about now that happened over five years ago. Neither situation would have had a different outcome in the end, with both animals being put to sleep but I still wonder if I could have given the pets a few more weeks to months if I had thought of a certain diagnosis sooner.

If any vet's mistakes cause actual harm or suffering, these are the occasions when the VDS will investigate further. If your track record is exemplary and you admit to your mistake, then there will be a mark on your record and nothing further. Unfortunately, there are vets or nurses that make far too many mistakes over their career and deserve further disciplinary action or to be struck off the register. You hear of stories via colleagues and vet friends of certain members of the profession that give treatment that is substandard; whether that is knowingly done or not. One of my friends wanted to 'whistleblow 'against another vet but was told that it could not be anonymous and she could then face legal action herself if that vet wanted to sue her for slander. This is the situation where we hope that no pets get hurt, that clients make many complaints and the vet does get struck off. We don't want to cover up for bad vets or nurses as they are the people who bring down the respect of the profession. We understand that in grief or anger, people will want to complain about a member of the profession and we don't discourage it as we want all pet care to be as good as it can be and for those who are truly responsible to be held to account. However, if all you're after is money, please do not hold an individual responsible and make the complaint about them as you are adding a lot of stress and worry, plus many sleepless nights, to a job that is already bad enough for this.

Obviously, on top of all of this we have a lot of the normal worries that everyone has about relationships, money, friends, family and general adult life. The good thing about our job being so busy most of the time is that you can forget most of those generic problems for hours at a time. The bad thing is that the only time you then have to focus on these things is when you're home and trying to sleep. My colleague who was told that the client wished 'she f****** died 'was, at that point, not sleeping much at all. She had her husband's family member in a coma recovering from major cancer surgery, having to support her husband through this time, whilst at the same time waiting for a major leak in their bathroom to be fixed, at the same time as trying to purchase their first home. She was barely holding it together and we kept telling her to take some time off but 'she didn't want to let us down and give us more work to do'. This is something we all say all the time to each other - we are a team and we are each other's support through a lot of things in life. Most of us would rather sacrifice our own health by coming to work even if we are poorly or haven't slept much, so long as we feel safe enough to look after the animals. The last thing we want to do is let down our colleagues or the pets we know have booked in specifically to see us that day. We are in this job because we are caring individuals and we put others above ourselves a lot of the time. As with all jobs, there are the times when a comment from one member of staff can upset another but these are often resolved very quickly when it turns out that something else happened in their day to put them on edge.

From the last two chapters, you can see why mental health issues amongst veterinary professionals are so high. According to a recent study by the Centres for Disease Control and Prevention, male vets are 2.1 times as likely, and female vets 3.5 times as likely to die by suicide compared to the general population. Other surveys imply the rates of suicide are up to four times higher in vets than other professions, and double that of doctors and dentists. The terrible stress and emotion that occurs in the job is the main reason for this. I can imagine these stresses occur just as much, and even more, for doctors. Owners of independent vet practices will often have major money troubles to add to the list of woes, which is why so many places are being bought by the corporates. Doctors in the NHS will not have these financial worries to the same level which may add to the discrepancy. As vets or vet nurses, we also have easy access to the drugs that are used for pet euthanasia and we see how peaceful that process is for the animals. As a practice, we have had to change the code to the dangerous drugs cupboard two additional times in my memory, purely due to worry about the mental health of two of our nurses.

These last two chapters have aimed to highlight the major issues within the profession. If you are feeling down or overwhelmed, there are many places to turn to. From friends and family to our specific vet helplines. You do not need to suffer alone. Every single vet will have felt as you do at some point in their career.

SAVING A LIFE

Yay! An uplifting topic. The last two chapters were originally posted during mental health week in the UK and are very important but yes, rather depressing. There are also amazing parts to our job; saving a life being one of them.

The majority of our job involves making ill animals feel better, or performing routine consultations like vaccinations and medication checks, or routine surgery. A lot of the time, the pets would get better on their own, but we can make them pain-free or feel better quicker than they would do without veterinary intervention. Anything that requires antibiotics is unlikely to resolve without our help but a skin infection or conjunctivitis is rarely life-threatening. Obviously, it will cause the animal discomfort and irritation, thus still very much better treated. Even seemingly more dangerous scenarios such as a broken leg are unlikely to cause death if untreated; the body will fix itself as best as it can and the leg may not be able to be used properly again, but the pet will survive, albeit in severe pain for the first few weeks. Obviously, in any situation like this we would strongly recommend veterinary intervention but we cannot claim to have saved a life. Only every few weeks will we actually physically save a life with our day's work, and there really is no better feeling.

The most common scenario for this to occur is when animals are hit by a car. Cats are more commonly hit by cars than dogs and unfortunately, a lot of the time they are killed outright and we have no time to intervene. In those occasions where they make it into us, they can range from being miraculously injury free and just in shock, to brain injuries, lung problems and internal organ damage. When in shock, the heart rate increases, the blood pressure decreases and only the vital organs get the blood supply. If the shock is severe, an animal can die because of this. To counteract the shock, we have to pump fluids into the body at a very fast rate and sometimes give drugs too.

One particularly memorable RTA (road traffic accident) involved a cat that had been hit on it's front end and was unconscious, with one eye hanging out of its socket, a broken jaw and had difficulty breathing. After placing an IV catheter, giving very strong painkillers, and giving it a bolus of fluids, the nurse and I let it breathe in some oxygen for a few minutes, whilst gathering information from the owner who we located using the microchip details. They hadn't been present when the cat had been hit and so had no idea what was happening until we called them and got permission to administer more than just pain relief and fluids (another good reason to get a cat microchipped - we are only legally allowed to perform 'first aid 'without the owner's consent).

Once the breathing rate had calmed down, we took an x-ray that showed a pneumothorax - air trapped in the 'pleural space 'between the lungs themselves and the chest wall. At this point, the cat started to show a little bit of brain function in that shining a light into its remaining eye caused the pupil to constrict which was a positive sign. We inserted a needle into the chest cavity and removed the air from the pleural space. The breathing rate decreased to a slightly more normal level but we kept the cat on oxygen for about another half an hour, giving fluids at the same time. Over the next 12 hours, the cat slowly regained consciousness due to some drugs that we gave to reduce the pressure in the brain. The breathing and heart rate came down to a much more manageable levels and we could then fix the far more obvious problems - proper removal of the eye, wiring of the fractured jaw and placing a feeding tube into the oesophagus. Another couple of days later, the cat was allowed to go home and went on to make a full recovery; it just couldn't catch as many mice now it only had one eye!

One of the most dramatic and sudden life-saving situations is saving an animal from internal bleeding. The most common presentation for this is a tumour of the spleen or liver that bursts inside the dog's abdomen. Obviously, if left for more than a few hours, depending on the amount of bleeding, this can be fatal. There are two of these scenarios that stay ingrained in my memory. The first one was when I was on call and it was one of the nurse's birthday meals out in town. A middle aged Labrador was being brought down because it was suddenly unable to get up and was breathing rapidly. When I saw the very pale gums and could hear a very high heart rate, I knew we needed to get the ultrasound machine out. The ultrasound showed an abdomen full of fluid and what appeared to be a tumour on the spleen. A quick needle into the abdomen showed that the fluid was blood and I went to chat to the owners. Splenic tumours are 50/50 benign versus malignant so if the dog is otherwise fit and well, we would always recommend surgery. There are complications that can occur and sadly, if malignant, the prognosis is only 3-6 months. However, in this 8 year old, normally springy Labrador, it was a no-brainer to try. He had lost a lot of blood into the abdomen and it was my nurse that kept him alive during the anaesthetic whilst I stopped the bleeding and removed the spleen. It was only after hearing a dripping noise that I realised that a lot of the blood that had been floating in his abdomen had spilt onto the operation table and was now dripping onto the floor and a large portion of it had soaked through my top and trousers.

We carried on, and after a few hours, he was stable and ok to be left for an hour whilst we went to quickly chomp down on our pre-ordered food at the restaurant with everyone else. I had brought a spare set of clothes with me, hoping to have made it to the whole birthday dinner, but hadn't thought I'd need a spare set of knickers. The blood had soaked through my trousers to my knickers so I had to go commando under my jeans! Sadly, the results of the analysis of this particular dog's tumour was not what we wanted and we had to put him to sleep a few months later. It does hit you harder as a vet when you have helped animals through very tricky situations, hoping that it will be enough, only for the pet to need to be put to sleep anyway. It doesn't stop us trying though! The second memorable splenic tumour bleed had a more positive outcome though I would never have guessed at the time. The German shepherd dog was about 13 years old, thin and very much looked her age, and it was a miracle that we got her through the anaesthetic. The most incredible thing was that the tumour was as big as my head (we have photos to prove it) and weighed 3.9kg, yet came back as benign! She was a much happier dog after the surgery and put weight on and is still alive and well a year later.

Something else we see all too often is a 'blocked bladder 'in male cats. This occurs when a stone or some severe inflammation in the bladder blocks the long, thin outlet of the male urinary system, meaning the bladder just gets bigger and bigger and is at risk of rupturing. As you can imagine from really needing to wee and not being able to find a toilet quickly, this is a very unpleasant feeling. The major threat to life is the increase in a substance called potassium in the bloodstream; when above a certain point it can cause the heart to stop. Therefore, we have to pass a urinary catheter reasonably quickly and place the animal on a drip and give medications to help bring the potassium down and help the kidneys.

Wombat was one such cat that we had in the hospital for quite a few days after his owner noticed he kept trying to go to the toilet in random areas in the house - something he had never done before. Once you remove the urinary catheter, you hope that the urethra will not block again. Poor Wombat did block again so was not allowed to go home and had to have another urinary catheter placed, some different drugs given and luckily it went to plan from there on out. Sadly, unless the underlying problem is resolved (often stress related), the blockage can recur in the near future. Interestingly, we have seen an increased number of blocked bladders over the past year or so; although the dogs may be happy to have owners working from home during the pandemic, the cats are stressed that we are invading their quiet home in the daytime! If you ever see your male cat straining to urinate without passing anything, please take it to a vet very quickly.

There are obviously many more scenarios where we can save an animal's life; a twisted stomach, congestive heart failure, a pyometra, a Caesarian, removal of a 'foreign body 'in the gut, severe pancreatitis, a very bad gut infection causing blood poisoning, a rabbit with gut stasis, removal of certain cancers, a diabetic or Addisonian crisis, breathing difficulties, heatstroke, the list goes on. Sometimes, these life-saving moments can only prolong a pet's life for months rather than years and sometimes, their lives cannot be saved for more than a few hours; enough to give a family time to say goodbye.

Occasionally, there are times when the life-saving can occur in a matter of moments. These are the situations where we have to perform CPR. If an animal 'crashes', it is often due to a reaction to an anaesthetic either because of a sensitivity to a drug or because they were so poorly that they weren't expected to survive the anaesthetic to start with. They can also 'crash 'as the last sequel to any of the aforementioned emergency situations, though luckily we tend to be able to intervene before this happens. Most people know about human CPR from TV programmes or first aid courses. The theory is the same with animals though small dogs, cats and smaller animals require chest compressions with the strength of your hand, not your whole body weight. In practice, we place a tube in the throat and attach them to oxygen and give them artificial breaths. There are many drugs that we can also give to aid the recovery of a heart beat. All vets and nurses are taught CPR from the start and it is something that most of us will instinctively start doing as soon as a heart stops. If it occurs during or straight after an anaesthetic, we do have a reasonable chance of success. It can be incredible when a pet dies and you bring it back to life again, all in the space of a couple of minutes; you hardly have time to catch your own breath or register what has happened, then you have to carry on with the surgery itself or wait for it to wake up fully, hoping it doesn't 'crash 'again. Sadly, if it is the end-point of an illness or trauma, it is rare for us to be able to bring pets back to life and if we do, they often die again, at which point we have to make a call as to whether it is fair to continue resuscitation.

On rare occasions in our profession, we have the ability and opportunity to save a human life, rather than an animal's. We are all taught to look out for signs of domestic abuse as there is a strong correlation between animal and human abuse. Personally, I have never experienced this but I know of colleagues who have. There is only one time that I may have contributed to saving a young teenage girl. She and her mother brought their cat in to see me that was very old and clearly very unwell; we could have put the cat through many tests to find out what was going on but she hadn't eaten for days, was very thin, dehydrated and was clearly suffering. The girl was so wise beyond her years, stating that she thought the best option for her beloved cat was to put her to sleep, even though for her sake she'd want to keep her alive. She realised that the most selfless act was to end the cat's suffering and the mother cried her eyes out and agreed.

The girl was very tall, slim and pretty but had braces and held herself in a posture that showed that she wanted to be smaller and not stick out so much. The mother asked her to go to get something from the car and whilst she was out, she broke down and said that her daughter was on suicide watch and was going through some terrible mental health issues due to being bullied at school. The mother was very concerned that the loss of her cat would push her over the edge. I didn't know what to say but exclaimed how sorry I was and the daughter came back into the room. She was such a lovely girl; polite and kind and it was clear that any bullying that was being done was out of jealousy of her intelligence and model stature. A few days after the death of a pet, we often write a sympathy card to the family. On this occasion, I enclosed a separate letter for the mother to give to her daughter, if she felt it appropriate. I wrote about what a wonderful girl I thought she was and that she was exactly the type of person who would make a great vet; that a lot of us vets were teased as we grew up for being a geek or know-it-all, that we were rarely the popular kids at school and that I hoped my words could go a small way to making her feel better. A few months later, the same mother came to me with their new kitten. The mother thanked me for my letter and told me that her daughter was a much happier girl now and wanted to be a vet when she grew up. I hope that I played a small part in that girl's happiness and she goes on to be stronger and more confident person.

We really do have a lot of responsibility on our shoulders by being a vet, and we really do our best to make as many lives better as we can. When we actually save a life, it is a level of emotion that is unmatched in a lot of things in life. In those times where you know that that animal goes out of the vet practice and has no reason not to go on to live a full life, it is the best feeling that we can ask for. We often will go home and tell our loved ones that we saved a life today. Not many jobs can offer such a feeling and although we have incredible lows in our jobs, nothing can ever take away that high.

A MOUTH FULL OF ROTTEN TEETH

Informative chapter alert! This one has a lot of information about pet's teeth and the (lack of) joy of dentistry. It isn't the most scintillating of chapters but if you have a pet, it should be quite useful for you.

Rather like our love of pus, we also take great satisfaction in pulling out rotten teeth. We always feel sorry for these animals that have clearly had toothache for a while but cannot tell their owners. Pets will eat through oral pain because it is a constant, dull ache and if they avoid chewing with the particularly painful teeth, they can eat reasonably well. Videos of cats and dogs eating have been slowed down to observe how they are actually eating. A lot of the time, they are picking the food up with their tongue and chucking it to the back of their mouth where they just swallow it without chewing. Obviously, some of the time this is because they are greedy animals that just want to get the food in their stomach as fast as possible. However, in pets that used to take their time and chew biscuits, they think this action is to bypass the sore teeth. The same can be said for those that chew on one side of their mouth only. We have lost count of the number of times we have performed dental work and the owners will say afterwards that they had no idea their cat or dog had toothache but they are so much happier now so they must have done! If anyone has ever had a sore tooth, it really is an unpleasant experience and something we would not wish upon our pets.

There are a few breeds of dog that have worse teeth than others. Anything that has a smaller mouth than it should has the same number of teeth (42), squashed into a much smaller space. Along with the typical brachycephalic breeds such as French bulldogs and pugs, this also includes chihuahuas, Shih Tzus and Yorkshire terriers. In all these situations, it is common to find that the teeth overlap over each other, or some are even turned sideways to fit in. This means that there are many tight, small pockets for food to collect in and the gums slowly recede, causing the roots of the teeth to become covered in tartar. For some reason, dachshunds and miniature poodles seem to have terrible teeth too despite having longer snouts. In a lot of these dogs, the little incisor teeth at the front are the first to become rotten and wobbly. These are the easiest teeth to remove as they only have one, small root. Any tooth that is wobbly is very satisfying to remove - it tends to take us minimal effort and you know you are helping the dog in removing something painful and irritating.

The next teeth that tend to become rotten are the smaller premolar teeth. These are the few teeth directly behind the big canine 'fang 'tooth. The small ones have two roots so we have to drill them in half before getting them out. At this point, we may have had a bit of a struggle removing one of the roots of the premolars if one root was rotten and the other one was fine, but at least this gives us a sense of achievement. This would be where we want an ordinary dental to stop as the rest of the teeth are an absolute pain to remove, most of the time.

The larger premolars or molars near the back of the mouth have three roots that you have to split up in the correct way to make sure you don't leave part of one root attached to another. Sometimes we have to remove these teeth because the tooth is so covered in tartar and is very rotten. In these scenarios, we may even be able to remove the tooth without splitting the roots - something that will very much bring a smile to our faces. Unfortunately, sometimes the tooth needs to come out because just one of the roots is unhealthy due to a tooth root abscess, for example. In these situations, it can be a lot trickier to get the more healthy root(s) out and we can spend a long time putting pressure on the root in the correct way to break the ligament that keeps the tooth in place. If we get the root out whole, we have a sense of triumph and hold it up with a 'ta-daaaa' (no, seriously, I actually do make that noise). Occasionally, the root will snap and we have a much more difficult job of hunting the root out and removing it. The most reliable way of doing this is to perform a 'surgical extraction 'where we make a flap of gum over the root, drill away the bone surrounding the root and then lift it out. This is the same way that we remove the large, canine tooth as the root of the canine is actually even bigger than the part of the fang that you can see in the dog's mouth. This process can still take us twenty minutes to remove just *one* tooth. If you have to do this with several teeth in the mouth then suddenly it can take two hours to perform a dental on one dog. This is why we are so happy when any of these bigger teeth are already wobbly and we can remove them easily!

The worst dogs to perform dentals on are the larger breeds and, for some inexplicable reason, greyhounds. In a lot of these dogs, the roots are 'ankylosed 'into the jaw. This essentially means that they are cemented in place and are very, very difficult to remove even if they are rotten and painful at the surface. If the tooth is fractured with the pulp cavity exposed, it *has* to be removed as that is very sore. However, it is an otherwise healthy tooth with two other roots, so it can take forty five minutes just to remove the *one* tooth.

In any situation with a dental, we find it terribly amusing and exasperating when owners ask us 'not to remove teeth, unless it is *really* necessary'. What do you think we do? Pull out healthy teeth for fun? Trust me, there is absolutely no way we would ever remove a tooth unless it was necessary! I have had to tag-team dental procedures with other vets before because there were just too many difficult teeth to remove. They really did need to come out but we just couldn't cope without a break. There is a phrase 'if in doubt, take it out 'that we will very much ignore when it comes to teeth. If there is any doubt and we think the tooth can be saved, we will leave it in the mouth to save our-selves some time, wrist ache, sweating and swearing.

This is even more so the case when it comes to the worst of teeth to remove - the lower canine tooth (I'm pretty sure every vet and nurse reading this just nodded their heads in agreement). As well as having a very large root, that root tip tends to stop only millimetres before the bottom of the jaw bone. This means that it is surprisingly easy to fracture a dog or cat jaw at this point. Our heart sinks if we see that this tooth needs to come out and we have to ring an owner in advance to tell them the risks of removing the tooth. Most of the time, we eventually get it out safely, but it takes a lot of time and patience. A few of my colleagues and I have fractured a jaw in the process of removing this tooth. A lot of the time, the jaw will heal itself with soft food and painkillers and the pet will barely notice because that tooth was so sore to begin with anyway. Sometimes though, the jaw needs to be repaired with a plate or wire. Thus, if the tooth is ac-tively wobbly and rotten to begin with, we can be much happier in removing it.

Cat dentals can also be pretty satisfying if the teeth are rotten, for all the same reasons as with dogs. Cats have fewer teeth (28) but they are obviously much smaller, meaning the roots are more fragile and the slightest bit of pressure in the wrong direc-tion can cause a root to snap. There is a situation with cat teeth where we actually do remove healthy teeth too - something called lymphocytic-plasmacytic stomatitis. This is an unusual condition where the cat has an overactive immune response to small amounts of plaque on the teeth, thought to be caused by a mix of viruses and allergies. There are a few medical treatments but most are not successful and the only way to solve a very painful mouth is to remove the majority of the teeth. These tend to have a two hour slot booked for the vets to do this and rival a greyhound dental as one of the worst things to see booked in!

Cats also get tooth lesions called Feline Odontoclastic Resorptive Lesions (FORLs). This means that the tooth starts to dissolve itself at the gum-line, where we can visualise a hole in the tooth, eventually exposing the pulp cavity. This is a very painful condition but given cats are so bad at showing pain or at allowing owners to look in their mouths, they often go unnoticed until checks at the vets. It is good practice to take X-rays of all the teeth in a cat's mouth when anaesthetised for a dental as this allows us to check if any FORLs are starting on any roots of other, apparently healthy teeth. We can then remove these teeth before they start to dissolve and become painful. This saves your cat another dental procedure in 6-12 months. Unfortunately, if your cat suffers from FORLs, it very well may need another dental procedure in the future anyway

Dental procedures will always include a scale and polish of the teeth that are to remain in the mouth. Cracking off the chunks of tartar and scaling the tooth back to a white colour bring us joy too, especially knowing that the pet's breath will smell much sweeter! When we see the tartar starting to build up in your pet's mouth, we will often recommend just a scale and polish to reduce the chance of teeth needing to be removed in the future. To prevent tartar build up as much as possible, we would always recommend trying to brush your pet's teeth from when it is very young. If this is not possible, there are certain powders you can put in the food or gel you can spread on the teeth or in the water. After any dental procedure, we would recommend this again if you haven't already done so, to try to prevent any further procedures in the future. There are certain dental chews on the market too which can be very good for those teeth that are used for chewing (if they actually chew it) but the incisors and canines are left out of this and the chews are very high in calories. Chewing on bones can be useful but we see more fractured teeth or splinters of bone in the gut causing issues in these scenarios so we don't tend to recommend it.

Dental procedures in animals obviously require an anaesthetic and this will make owners reluctant to book their pets in, especially in the older animals. It is always better to sort the problem out whilst the pet is otherwise healthy and well. If the teeth get so sore and infected that the pet just cannot face eating anymore, then we have no choice but to perform the dental procedure. By this time, the anaesthetic risk becomes higher because they are even older and may have concurrent illnesses, as well as dehydration from not eating for the prior few days. Older patients tend to have a drip for the procedure and we perform pre-operative bloodwork to check that their organ function is still good before giving any drugs. This keeps the risk to a minimum and is a very good idea, despite the extra cost that is sometimes involved. I cannot remember ever losing a pet during a dental procedure - even the fifteen year old dog with bad heart diseases made it through. There have been a couple of times that the animal has 'crashed 'and we had to perform CPR, remove just the worst of the teeth and wake it up quickly but they have gone on to make a full recovery. Obviously, there are always exceptions and animals can have reactions to an anaesthetic but that risk is about 1 in 10,000. Would you prefer to live the rest of your life with tooth ache or take that risk though? People are also reluctant to pay for dental work because they think that their pet is fine as it is. Given the length of time your pet is under anaesthetic for, having us work on it's teeth, dentals are often very reasonably priced as we know that if we charged for our time more appropriately, the costs would be too high for people to book them in.

It makes us very happy when we have turned a sore mouth into a healthy mouth and owners come in for their post op check 10 days later and tell us how happy their pet now is. I often think we should have a 'dental book 'to show clients to persuade them to have dental work performed on their pet, full of previous owner comments about how their twelve year old now acts like a puppy and, of course, that their breath doesn't smell anymore.

GUINEA PIGS

This may seem like a strange title compared to a lot of the others but there is method to my madness. As vets, we get asked our opinion on children's pets only very occasionally and it is something we wished was discussed more often. Sometimes, families cannot commit to the care of a dog or cat because they don't fit in with their lifestyle and the costs associated with them, yet young children will want a pet. In this situation, our top recommendation is always a guinea pig. Yes, a guinea pig *not* a rabbit. Guinea pigs tend to be very easy to handle, don't bite very often and can respond well to cuddles from owners. We know plenty of people who have had guinea pigs in their adult lives too because of the fun interaction with owners. They each have their different personalities and habits, often squeaking in excitement when it is time for their favourite food. They are much, much happier in a pair or trio which means that they can entertain each other too and children can watch them interacting. The pair should consist of two or three females, or a male and a female or two - so long as the male is neutered. Two male pigs may start to fight as they become older, though if they are neutered and raised together from birth, this is less likely to happen.

The best thing about them is that they are much easier to care for than rabbits. Guinea pigs need a reasonably big cage, with suitable bedding such as recycled paper pellets or shredded paper. They need a section for playing and running, plus another part with a shelter for sleeping or getting out of bad weather. All of this can be bought at any good pet shop. The happiest pigs are those that are brought inside for the cold winter and taken outside in spring. However, so long as plenty of bedding is provided and a heat source on very cold nights, they can be kept outside all year round. Cages must be secure from wildlife and not on ground that becomes too wet.

The most common problems we see in pigs are to do with their food and environment. Lots of hay and grass should be provided, along with leafy greens to give good fibre and nutrient intake. If they do not have enough hay or grass, their teeth can become overgrown and need filing down by a vet. They only need a small amount of fruit and vegetables and it is best to avoid the sugary ones. To make sure they receive all the correct nutrients, such as vitamin C, they should also be given guinea pig pellets. It is very easy to overfeed this part of the diet and this tends to be the fattening bit too; half an egg cup full a day per pig is sufficient. A lot of pigs become butternut squash shaped as they are obese! This can make them more susceptible to other diseases, just like in cats and dogs. It is also best to use pellets rather than the cereal alternatives. You know those multi-coloured concoctions with some green blobs and some flattened oaty bits? Pets are silly and will just pick out the bits they like and leave the rest, meaning they miss out on key nutrients. If the bedding is too dusty, they can get some dust or sawdust in the eye; they can also inhale the dust and get a respiratory infection. This is why paper based beddings can be better.

Being outside a lot, they can also get parasites such as mites and fleas so need to be treated for these every so often. They can also get the occasional virus from other wildlife that causes pneumonia or diarrhoea but this tends to be very rare. Thus, a lot of their problems are easily preventable with good husbandry. They don't need any annual vaccinations and their fur is thicker and generally doesn't require grooming, unlike rabbits. They live for four or five years on average, so can be there for a lot of a child's younger life. As sad as it is for a pet to pass away, it can be a good situation in which to teach children about this tricky subject in life.

Rabbits share a lot of the same husbandry techniques as guinea pigs but are prone to many more health problems. Just like with guinea pigs, they can get dental disease though they tend to be worse in rabbits; we have to regularly perform dentals to burr down the overgrown teeth which becomes a repetitive issue for the bunny. They are very susceptible to 'gut stasis' which is a life-threatening condition where the guts stop moving. Any rabbit that hasn't eaten for twelve hours needs to be seen by a vet as soon as possible and they sometimes require hospitalisation, which can become costly. It can occur due to dental disease, an impaction in the guts, a response to any pain elsewhere in the rabbit, or just feeling unwell. Sometimes, even a fright from a fox out in the garden can trigger an episode of gut stasis! Honestly, bunnies can be an absolute nightmare. They can also get something called 'fly strike'. This is where blowflies come and lay eggs on moist areas around their bottom, which then hatch into maggots. These maggots then start to eat away at the skin and into the muscle and anus of the rabbit. We see this reasonably often in the summer and it is one of the most disgusting things to deal with and we feel so sad for the bunny. A lot of rabbits will not survive due to the toxins released into the blood stream from the maggots. Imagine dying from maggots eating your bum; it is bad enough for us having to pick them all off so goodness knows how the poor bunny must feel. We can sometimes save them if they are not too ill before they come into us so checking your rabbit's bottom twice daily for little white grains of rice (fly eggs) or maggots is a good idea. There are preventative sprays and creams you can use too and making sure the cage is kept clean and dry is good too. Most owners are unaware of this problem when they get a rabbit and can be faced with a very poorly bunny and unexpected vet bills. Although guinea pigs could potentially get this problem too, I've never seen it happen.

Rabbits do also like to be in pairs and we most commonly recommend a mixed pair that are then neutered. Up to 60% of female rabbits over the age of three will develop uterine cancer so it is always a good idea to get them spayed, no matter if you have a male or not. Guinea pigs can also get these cancers but they tend to occur later in their lives. Rabbits should live to 9-12 years old, so much more of a commitment to make. Rabbits have a very young socialisation period at 10-21 days old so if they have not been handled by the breeder, they can be very skittish and jump out of owner's arms very easily which is near impossible to rectify. This leads to a lot of rabbits that are ignored at home because they aren't friendly enough to bother playing with. I have had one male rabbit try to box me whilst clipping it's nails - so much so that we had to abandon the attempt. Pretty amusing image for you all I'm sure, vet versus rabbit and the rabbit winning! I had a particularly flighty bunny jump off my table in the consult room once; it seemed fine at the time but came back in a couple of hours later with a nosebleed which luckily stopped with some anti-inflammatory painkillers. I have only ever examined skittish rabbits on the floor since then!

Then you have all of the other common 'small furries' such as hamsters and gerbils. A lot of these are not handled properly when young so can bite quite easily. I think I have been bitten or had the hamster attempt to bite me in most of my consults with them so if asked, we would always say to avoid these unless handled properly from birth. We do see the occasional rat and they actually do make very good pets too. They tend to be very friendly and their main health concern is something called mycoplasma that causes a pneumonia. Unfortunately, public perception of rats is that they are pests so they aren't that popular. Some children are keen on reptiles and amphibians but these do require a lot of special care and attention and we would never encourage them as a pet for a child.

We don't see guinea pigs at the vets very often as they tend to be quite healthy, but we are always pleased to see them when we do as they are very cute. So if you are thinking of getting a pet that requires less work and commitment, no matter your age, please do think about a couple of guinea pigs.

GOING ABOVE
AND BEYOND

There are situations if veterinary life where vets, nurses and reception staff will go above and beyond our duty of care to deliver service that is exceptional. Yeah, yeah, here I am blowing our trumpet again (it's not just my own trumpet, but that of most vet staff I know) but recently there seems to be a constant barrage of abuse aimed at vets in the newspapers. Let's try to argue again that vets are not just in it for money.

These situations where we go above what is expected of us range from small acts of kindness to much more than that. It can be just because clients or pets are particularly lovely to us and we happen to not be as busy that day, if a client or pet finds themselves in a tricky or sad circumstance, or if they are clients that we have built up a relationship with over many visits. This can be something as simple as dropping medication directly to somebody's door if their pet is on long term drugs and the owner is unwell. We can squeeze in extra consults between fully booked sessions, knowing it will mean our lunch break is shortened or we all go home later. It can be calling somebody with results a day earlier than expected because you asked the lab to process it urgently. A couple of times I have stayed late to call owners who I knew had issues with anxiety and wouldn't sleep with the worry of their pet's blood results, even though I only took them a few hours ago and told them I'd call the next day.

We have clients that will call several times over problems that we know aren't an issue with the pet, just that owners are overly worried or anxious people. In this situation, we don't want to take their money unnecessarily so members of staff will take time out to speak to then in turn, reassuring them that everything is fine. The best examples of these are from a young lady who had got herself a dog to help with her anxiety issues. Sadly, this seemed to give her something to *focus* all her worries onto. Unfortunately, she picked a German shepherd which can be neurotic enough if not exercised and stimulated sufficiently but with her own issues projected onto him, he was certainly difficult to examine. We would take time in the consult to feed him treats and slowly get near enough to him, little by little, to be able to examine any part of him. One wrong move and he'd cry and go to hide behind his owner. This then increased her anxiety further and the cycle continued. It meant that the slightest issue with him was then an extreme situation in the owner's eyes. We would see him for a mild illness such as one bout of diarrhoea that we would examine him for, work out that he was well in himself and then have several days worth of phone calls every few hours with updates about his faeces and questions about whether that is fine or not. We once had him rushed into us because he had a lump on his testicle. Turns out it was the head of the epididymis, a completely normal lump to be on the testicle that will have been there the whole time, the owner will just not have seen it from that angle before. After reassuring her of this, we still had many phone calls about it over the next few days, We do all we can to help clients like this as we know it is an illness in itself, but it is certainly a situation of 'treating the owner, rather than the pet'.

Another similar circumstance was with Mrs King, an elderly lady who lived alone with her old spaniel, who's husband had passed away and who didn't have any children or friends to look after her. Every staff member knew the whole story of her life because she would tell anyone who she was on the phone to. She was clearly very lonely and had worried about most things all her life, meaning she was very emotional. We had saved her phone number in the 'on call 'phone so we knew who it was and could prepare ourselves before answering the call. These calls would be at least twenty minutes long, starting with her crying and telling you about the latest problem with Robbie the spaniel, and ending with her life story again and us trying to calm her down. Some of the reasons for calling do make us laugh after the phone call though. For example, she has called me before because she ran over Robbie's tail with the vacuum. Once establishing it wasn't bleeding at all, I asked her what he was doing now. She told me that he was stood there looking at her and wagging his tail. Obviously, this showed that no bad damage had occurred but it took me a long time to stop her crying and go make herself a cup of sugary tea.

Another time, she called to say that she couldn't find Robbie's steroid tablet that he was on for his skin issues. She was hysterical, exclaiming that she had put it out on the side before making her lunch and what would happen if she accidentally ate it in her cream cheese sandwich? I advised that a one off, tiny dose would be unlikely to cause her any harm even with the very small chance that she had eaten it, and that Robbie could be given a tablet now instead. My colleagues have had similar calls, with her once asking with the change of clock time overnight, should she give his tablets at the new 8pm or the old one? The reception team will often be on the phone for ages in the daytime, also trying to work out whether Robbie had an actual issue that he needed to be seen for, or whether it was just another phone call to try to calm Mrs King down. We have recommended charity phone lines to these clients several times as we are not qualified to counsel people but we feel that speaking to them ourselves can go a small way to help.

As previously mentioned, we have a lot of tragic circumstances surrounding pets, where the pet means more to an owner than a normal pet-owner relationship. They are links to lost family members or doted on like the children they could never have. We often go beyond the care expected of us in these situations. Some of the nurses have given their phone numbers to certain clients to arrange pet sitting services so they know their pets are in the best hands whilst they are away. Reception staff will block out double appointments with the clients so the vets can take more time in the consult, knowing that there will be many questions and tests to be performed immediately, just for the owner's peace of mind - asked for by the owner by the way, not insisted on by the vet. Vets will forgive any readings of search engines online, knowing that this will partly be the reason for their worry given any vague clinical sign means instant death or cancer according to the internet. Sometimes these owners will write pages of an email or letter, just to let us know the latest development in any clinical signs which we will try to respond to in a timely manner.

Occasionally we will suggest or do certain things that puts ourselves out, because the owner doesn't have enough money and we cannot bear to see any animal suffer because of this. I have lost count of the number of times we have given certain treatments at reduced costs to avoid owners having to make difficult decisions. For example, I can remember a time when a chihuahua got a piece of a bone stuck in her oesophagus. It had been lodged there for over 24 hours, she couldn't eat and was struggling to breathe. Due to the risk of damage, we couldn't just push the bone into the stomach and remove it from there as it was likely to tear the whole oesophagus. Instead, she needed her chest opening and the piece of bone removing from a carefully made incision that is sutured back again. This is a specialist level surgery and should costs many thousands which the owner could not afford. We didn't have the time to wait for charities to respond to the owner about donations, so my boss advised that he would attempt the surgery himself at cost price. He had never performed this surgery before which he made very clear to the owner, the dog would have to be ventilated throughout the operation, there were many post-op complications possible and all these were made more likely given his inexperience with the operation. This was part of the reason he felt we couldn't charge more than cost price. It was still a reasonable amount of money but the owner was very grateful given the dog would die if we didn't try. Amazingly, she survived it all and went home happily!

We have also performed a number of leg amputations in animals who have had broken legs and the owner could not afford any repair. An amputation is a much cheaper procedure and requires a much shorter recovery period, meaning the animal can be happily running around on three legs after a couple of weeks. Even though it is cheaper, many people cannot afford that either so we have done many procedures at cost price. There is a very big difference between being unwilling to pay for something, and being unable to pay for it and we do make sure of our decision before going ahead with these procedures. Still, it is something we do to stop animals suffering as a result of owner's misfortune or lack of planning.

The time of day that we perform operations can also make a difference to an owner's bill. There was one weekend at about midday when an owner brought in her papillon dog who had been unwell for a few days, was not eating and was vomiting but drinking excessively. Her temperature was very high and she was not spayed, meaning I quickly performed an ultrasound scan and confirmed she had a pyometra and needed surgery to remove the womb. Normally, we would put an ill dog on a drip for a few hours before anaesthetising them, to stabilise their blood pressure. Unfortunately, that would have taken us into 'out of hours 'as I had fully booked consults on this Saturday afternoon between 2-4pm so could not perform the surgery then. Anything after 4pm counted as 'out of hours'. This would increase the bill by a couple of hundred pounds and the owner made it clear, in a very nice manner, that she couldn't really afford the operation to start with, let alone the OOH fees. The nurse and I therefore gave her a quick bolus of fluids to make her feel better, then took her to surgery over our lunch break instead, so that the owner didn't have to pay the OOH fees. It is not legal to work an 8 hour day without an hour lunch break but we did it anyway, as we so often do in veterinary medicine, because we care more about the animals and their owners than ourselves.

Then we have those animals and owners that we build up a bond with because we see them regularly or our personalities just click instantly. When we have these relationships, we are likely to go even further beyond what is expected of us. There are three separate occasions I can remember when I have come in on my time off to put pets to sleep who I was very fond of and had become close to the owners of. The first one, Benny, a beloved and loving 3 year old golden retriever who had unexplained abdominal pain and wasn't responding to any treatment that we tried. The owner, Miss Barnaby, was a lady who I have mentioned before, who I used to gossip about dates with. We had become close when I went on a house visit to PTS her first retriever and since then, she had brought her dogs to me for all their routine treatment. Poor Benny was in pain that was only placated with strong opioid drugs; none of us could work out what was wrong with him despite many x-rays, blood tests, scans and surgery but we assumed a cancerous cause.

After I left work that day, on our early 5pm finish, his condition deteriorated and the vet who I handed him over to called me to say that she had discussed things with the owner and that she was coming in to put him to sleep. There was no doubt in my mind that I was going to come in to be there for the owner and for poor Benny in his final minutes. After taking my dinner back out of the oven, I drove back into the practice and the relief on the owner's face when she saw me told me that I had made the right decision to come back in. She was so grateful to me for coming in on my own time, and couldn't bear to think it was not going to be me putting Benny to sleep. The thing that owners probably don't realise is that we also want it to be ourselves putting these pets to sleep. I wanted to be there to let Benny go; he knew me and trusted me and it would make his final moments that bit better to have me there rather than a stranger, no matter how wonderful that stranger is. I also wouldn't have been able to sleep that night, knowing that I hadn't been there for my friend, Miss Barnaby, thus it was as much for me as it was for her. We hugged and cried on each other, me trying to stay strong for her sake. Poor Benny hadn't had a long enough life but at least the time he had been with is owner was filled with love. Something I always like to remind owners of in these situations is that the pet doesn't know that it has died early in life - all they know is that they had some time on this earth that was, hopefully, full of love and fun and then they were very poorly and now they aren't here any more. I would like to think that this helps owners through these tough times.

The other two situations were reasonably similar except for the fact that both pets were much older and had chronic issues that we had been treating for months. One was Mrs Meridale, who I have discussed previously as we used to share recommendations about gin. Poor Chloe, the pug, had an oral tumour and over a few months had become very unwell. When the time came to put her to sleep, it was a weekend and I wasn't working but her favourite nurse was. Chloe had been coming to see the nurse for her nail clips and to see me for her health care. I was free at the time so came into the practice and we both went to Chloe's house to put her to sleep and she drifted off peacefully. On another day off, I drove to a client's house to put her cat, Maria, to sleep. She was the cat who used to lick water off her owner when she got out the shower and bat the objects off the arm of the sofa as if playing a game. She had chronic kidney disease and had lost a lot of weight and now her appetite too. With cats, we can give them an injection of a sedation to make them unconscious and unaware of anything past that point. Their kidneys are very easily found on palpation and we can inject the overdose of anaesthetic into them, rather than placing an IV catheter which requires the aid of a nurse. The owner had previously requested that this was the method to be used, so that it could just be me that came to the house on my own. Due to safety reasons, we never normally do this but given it was on my own time and with a client I knew very well, we made the exception and for all of this, the owner was very grateful.

I am not alone in coming in on my time off to help with a case or put to sleep a pet. Most of my colleagues have done the same thing and I know my friends who work in other practices have done similar. One of my bosses is the only one who can perform certain orthopaedic surgeries in our practice and I have lost count of the times he has come in on a day off so that the pet wasn't left another day without its operation. My brother has stayed behind for several hours after work to perform an operation for one of his clients, and then gone back in in the middle of the night to check up on it. All of these things that I have discussed are *unpaid.* We do not get a single penny for this extra work. The nurses are no different, with most of them using their time off occasionally to be there for an owner or pet that they have also formed a bond with. Those that have given their numbers to clients for pet sitting services are also messaged a lot about health issues too and will text one of us for advice if they don't know the answer themselves. A lot of us are friends with some of our close clients on social media and are happy to help them with questions about their pet's care. When one of Mrs Meridale's pugs was having a night of seizures post toxin ingestion, her favourite nurse slept on the kennel floor with the pug all night in case she started to fit again. All these things are not asked for or expected of us; we offer to do them because we all care about the pets and the nice clients who we know will appreciate what we do. So the next time anyone wants to write a comment on an article about how vets are only in it for the money, have a read of this.

GETTING A 'THANK YOU'

When we have treated a pet and the outcome is positive, we often get a 'thank you 'said at the end of the consultation or on discharge from the hospital. It is always nice to hear those words and to know that we are appreciated. It can be something as simple as managing to clip a cat's nails when the owners can't manage it themselves, or feeling a lump and telling owners that it is a benign fatty lump or cyst rather than the cancer they feared.

Occasionally, if we have had the animal in the hospital or performed surgery to help the pet get better, owners take the time to write us a 'thank you' card and this really does mean a lot to us. I know a lot of vets have a box that they keep their 'thank you' cards in, or we put them up in the staff room so that everyone can have a read. Often, they are addressed to the vets, nurses and support staff as we all contribute to the health of the pet and the reason why they have got better. From the receptionist knowing on the phone that a problem that may not seem too serious to an owner is actually something to be seen quickly, to the nurses who give exceptional care and pick up on subtle signs that a pet is improving or deteriorating and to us vets that then make and perform plans accordingly; we all have a part to play. For any new vet or nurse to be given this compliment and assurance that their work was good and their communication skills were as they should be, can be a real confidence boost. The lovely words that people write can lift your mood and your day can turn from one where you feel stressed and down, to happy and well-liked. It really does put a smile on your face to know that we are appreciated. Sometimes, the 'thank you' card will be a collage of photos of the pet, and is often signed off as though the pet itself wrote it which is always adorable. If there are children in the family, we often get hand-drawn (and hilarious) pictures of the pet with the vet. I remember a certain card we were given where the mum of the family had to expressly tell me that the rather phallic shaped object the daughter had drawn on the dog's leg was meant to be the wound that we had stitched up. Cue a lot of giggles from a lot of us and the card being pinned to our staff room board for many months. Rarely, people even take the time to send us poems they have found or made up about us.

We will sometimes get boxes of chocolates or biscuits to share amongst the staff which always goes down very well! Those that have baking talents will make us homemade cakes which are usually gone within a few hours. One of my colleagues is constantly made a selection of desserts or cakes by one of her lovely clients, who insists she is too skinny and must be fed more (she isn't; these clients are just a bit more curvy and think everyone else should be so too)! We have a wonderful couple who will bring us a box of biscuits or chocolates every time they bring one of their many cats in for a procedure; even if it is a routine treatment such as a dental, they are so appreciative that their cats are happier than they were previously that they will always bring something at the post-op check. The excitement from any of the staff when they see such treats brought in would be enough to show clients how much it means to us. Individuals may be given bottles of wine or bunches of flowers from extremely generous clients and we will find it hard to suppress our gratitude and act in a professional way only. It doesn't look particularly professional to well up and hug the client but that's what we feel like doing. I will always tell my parents when I receive a gift like this as it hopefully makes them proud that I am doing well at a job that they encouraged and happy that they supported me through my studies.

If you are lucky enough to build up relationships with clients, each Christmas you receive many cards and festive treats. A few years ago, I treated a cat for a very strange ear disease that I knew wasn't normal and referred to a specialist. They instantly knew what it was and how to treat it so sent him back to me to perform said treatment. Apparently only a couple of cats per year are diagnosed with the condition but the way it presents is obvious when you have seen it once. Ever since then, the owners have given me a bottle of bubbly every Christmas, even if I have only seen the cat for its vaccination that year. They were so worried about their cat at the time and were just so happy that in referring them to the right person, their cat made a full recovery - even though it wasn't me that actually knew of the disease! Mrs Meridale, previously mentioned with the pugs and poor Chloe, gives me a selection of gins each Christmas so we can compare notes the next time we see each other.

Strangely, we get many more people more saying 'thank you' after a PTS than after making an animal better. We think it is because it is always such an emotional time that an owner dreads (as we all know from personal experience) and they are just so grateful when the process goes as smoothly as it can. The cards that we get sent will often make us cry due to the kind words and emotions that came from the situation. The nurses are prized for their compassion and gentle ways and they are often thanked alongside the vet. The gifts we receive can often be more lavish than at any other time. I have received various vouchers for certain retailers of very generous value and lots of different alcohols or beautiful bunches of flowers. One of my colleagues received a whole case of wine from a high end brand after a particularly emotional PTS with one of his clients. A few of us have been given framed photos of the lost pets that are kept on office desks or in the staff room. My most treasured present came from Miss Barnaby, with Benny who had to be PTS far too soon in life. This was one of the occasions where I came in despite my shift having finished that day. Knowing full well that I wouldn't get any extra pay or time off for coming in on my own time (not that I would expect to), she wanted to let me know how much she valued the fact that I did. She bought me a silver necklace with a small, heart shaped locket enclosed with angel wings. She says this is because I was her angel that day and that is something I will never forget. I am actually wearing the necklace as I write this.

In this modern age, there is another way that people can show their respect and admiration for what the practice, or individual, does. This is by giving a good review on social media or search engines. It is always very heartening to hear what people think of us and you can often find references to it on our group mobile chats, letting us all know that another lovely review has been posted. When you see a bad review, it can make you very upset and question what you did as a practice. Luckily for us, on social media any one bad review is often greeted with a barrage of comments underneath from our loving, loyal clients who will retell their stories of the times we have been exceptional in our care. To know that these clients not only appreciate what we do, but are willing to get into arguments about it really does hit home to us how our jobs can make a difference to people. I call it a 'job' but a lot of the time, it is a lot more than that and we will never tire of people thanking us.

So if you do feel like you are happy with your vet practice's care, please do let them know in whatever way you would like to. Once you've paid your bill with us, we understand that most people don't want to spend more money on presents but it costs nothing to send us an email or leave a review. Receiving presents is always a lovely bonus but reading or hearing kind words can make all the difference to us and remind us why we do this job.

A TOXICITY CASE

There are a range of substances that are not safe for animals to eat; some well known and some that are slightly more obscure. When we know that the animal has eaten such a substance, and how much, it is one of the rare cases in veterinary medicine where we know right from the start what the plan of action is. We like these cases because the majority of the time, we can get the pet well and home in 24-48 hours and follow a set protocol that means our job is that little bit easier.

In most situations, we start by making the pet vomit. In dogs, this is usually rather straightforward - we inject them with something that acts on the vomiting centre in the brain and within ten minutes, up comes the stomach contents. The vomiting tends to continue for fifteen or twenty minutes, with one of us holding the container and trying to get the dog to vomit into it and not all over the floor. Rather like the times you hold back your best friend's hair as she vomits due to drinking too much, we often have to hold back the floppy, hairy ears of the dogs so that they don't get vomit all over them. Sometimes, we tie them back with a bit of bandage! We once had a dog in that had eaten a rat that had been poisoned with rat poison; he was then made to vomit and brought it up *whole*. Why don't dogs chew their food? We sometimes have to induce vomiting when the dog has eaten bits of plastic or metal that the owner is worried will get stuck in the intestines. This means the vets and nurses have to sift through the vomit to make sure that it has all come up. I was once presented with a dog that had eaten all the contents of a dustbin and shortly afterwards, started to become very wobbly and was falling all over the place so the owners knew he must have eaten something toxic but didn't know what. We made him vomit and then had to look through the sick to see what could have been the cause. Turns out, he had eaten about 40 teabags which was enough caffeine to cause the clinical signs. Obviously, the tea bags were still whole. Being kept overnight on a drip flushed all the rest of the caffeine out of his system and he was back to normal in the morning.

It is much more difficult to make a cat sick as the drug that works in dogs doesn't affect cats. Thankfully, cats are slightly less stupid than dogs and most of them will avoid things that aren't good for them. However, they do have a penchant for eating bits of plants - the worst one being lilies. Ironic that my cat is called Lily, right? Lily toxicities are one of the few toxicities that we don't like seeing because it invariably causes kidney failure. Just grooming themselves after brushing past the pollen can be enough to cause serious damage. Unfortunately, a lot of the time owners don't know that the cat has done so and they only come into us once they are already poorly, by which time it is too late. On the rare occasion that the owner knows they have eaten some of the plant, we have a couple of drugs that can make them sick but none are reliable enough to work every time. Picture us putting the cat in its carrier and spinning it round and round in the hope that it will help. A young cat came to see me once because it had eaten garlic capsules which contained a toxic dose. Most cats and dogs can get away with eating a clove or two if they so desire, but the capsules that humans take for various health reasons have a very high dose that can cause destruction of the pet's red blood cells. No matter how hard we tried, we couldn't get this cat to be sick so we ended up giving it a very quick anaesthetic to flush its stomach instead.

Other dose-dependent toxicities include onions (they are the same family as garlic), various plants and bulbs and, of course, chocolate. People tend to panic over chocolate but there are quite a lot of toxicity calculators online that you can use. Large dogs have to eat a lot of chocolate before it becomes a problem. I had a call on Easter Sunday one year to tell me that their 50kg American Bulldog had just eaten an easter egg including two chocolate bars inside, a packet of sugar-coated chocolate eggs and some white chocolate buttons. Given it was all milk chocolate or less and the dog was so big, this didn't even reach the toxic level. However, if a chihuahua ate even a square of dark chocolate, this would be the time to bring it to the vets. We make them sick and if we are convinced that most came up, we will likely send the pet home with some activated charcoal to soak up the toxins in the guts before they enter the blood stream. If we are worried, we will admit them to be placed on a drip to support the kidneys and liver whilst the body processes the theobromine in the chocolate. When you've seen and smelt chocolate flavoured dog vomit many times, it rather ruins chocolate for you.

Pretty much everyone knows about chocolate being bad for pets but a less well known toxin is xylitol, something that is used as a sugar alternative in chewing gums, sweeteners, toothpaste and even some brands of peanut butter. Humans don't release insulin in response to xylitol but dogs and cats do, meaning they have very low blood sugar levels within an hour of ingestion. A lick of toothpaste is likely to be fine but a few pieces of chewing gum will probably need medical intervention. More than this, and your pet may go into liver failure. To combat this risk, after inducing vomiting, we will again put these dogs on fluids and give charcoal, liver support drugs and monitor the glucose levels closely.

Some human foods, such as raisins and grapes, are not dose dependent and are what we call *idiosyncratic reactions*. This means some dogs or cats can eat a whole punnet of grapes and be fine, whilst others just have to eat a few raisins (such as in hot cross buns, fruit cakes and biscuits) to go into kidney failure. We have no way of knowing which your dog or cat is unless they have eaten them before, but we think only a very small percentage of animals actually do react. My friend who works in a referral centre says they will see a few cases a year of pets that have indeed gone into kidney failure but personally, I have never seen this happen.

Some substances have specific antidotes that we have to use. Rat poison stops the body being able to clot the blood by taking away a clotting factor called vitamin k. This means that over the next few days, a dog or cat will start to bleed internally and you may see signs on the outside. If we know a pet has eaten rat poison long enough ago that inducing vomiting won't help, we start them on vitamin k injections and tablets. If a cat eats paracetamol, they cannot break it down as they lack the enzyme in their body and they go into liver failure. We can give them something called acetylcysteine to combat this. A low dose of paracetamol in dogs is completely safe and encouraged as pain relief; strange how some animals are able to eat things and others aren't. Then we have the best antidote of all, the antidote to anti-freeze. Anti-freeze is toxic to both dogs and cats due to the ingredient ethylene glycol. Anti-freeze tastes sweet so if there is any that drips onto the floor after defrosting your car, or from a spilt container, the animals will go for it. Once ingested, the ethylene glycol causes damage to the kidneys very rapidly so there isn't too much time to make them vomit though we still try. Left untreated, animals will go into renal failure and it is fatal after a few days. However, there is an antidote that can lead to a much better prognosis. The medical version is fomepizole but this is very costly and not widely available. The cheaper and fantastic alternative is ethanol - of which there is a high concentration in any hard, clear spirits you can get in the supermarket. We have a bottle of vodka in the cupboard for exactly this purpose (not for us when we have a bad day).

The most memorable occasion is when we had a cat and a small terrier in our kennels for three days, on drips that were spiked with vodka. The cat had about two shots into its veins over the course of treatment and the dog had double this. Obviously, this does get them drunk which can be pretty entertaining for us to see. I can remember that the cat became very happy, purring and constantly falling asleep in that head nodding way you see near the end of a night out. The dog was definitely a hungry drunk, gobbling down anything we put in his kennel which the owner said was unusual for him. This story had a happy ending and both pets went home with no lasting damage. Sadly, these things all require owner knowledge that the pet has eaten them. Unfortunately, we have seen quite a few cases of presumed anti-freeze toxicity that we didn't start to treat until 48 hours post ingestion, by which time it is too late and even with days of supportive care for the kidneys, the animals stop producing urine and die from the toxins going around the body. Dogs that present days after eating rat poison will likely need blood transfusions and a drip to keep them alive, rather than just an antidote. When spaying a dog once, we found that she had a very enlarged spleen and the whole operation was very oozy and the blood wasn't clotting properly. Unfortunately, unbeknownst to us, the owners had seen her eating rat poison the previous week and she bled out and died, despite our best efforts to save her.

Then we have the drug toxicities - from overdosing with animal drugs to pets being given human drugs. Sometimes this can be from pets being idiots and eating things you wouldn't expect them to, such as psoriasis cream that causes vitamin D toxicity. A lot of human drugs are safe at small levels but if a normal human dose is administered to a dog or a cat, this can be a large overdose. A miniature poodle once stole just one 400mg ibuprofen sugar-coated tablet which was a five times overdose, especially as animals are particularly susceptible to ibuprofen toxicity. He was in the hospital for five days on every antacid we could find and a drip to support his kidney function; his kidney parameters rose after a few days but then came down again and luckily subsequent blood tests have shown there to be little lasting damage. Dogs and cats have their own versions of ibuprofen that we give as anti-inflammatory pain relief and they are fantastic drugs that can turn an old Labrador into a bouncing six year old again. However, they are reasonably easy to overdose by giving them twice daily rather than once daily, or misreading the label and giving a 60kg dose rather than a 6kg dose. Occasionally, some dogs will just have a reaction to it that causes bloody vomiting and diarrhoea (similar to humans and ibuprofen apparently). We note this on their file so as to not use that class of drugs again, which is a shame because they really are the best painkillers we have for long term use. Also, if the pet already has liver or kidney disease, we have to be cautious as the drugs can exacerbate this, though they have only been shown to actually cause this disease if given in an already dehydrated animal. Therefore, we sometimes have to have pets in on the same supportive care as with ibuprofen. Flea treatment can also be a problem if overdosed or given to the wrong species. We once had a cat come in who had been given a dog flea product - this was not the owner's fault as the label from the shop-bought product said it could be used for cats too. Sadly, the cat was fitting and despite 24 hours of care, she didn't improve and her organs failed. Certain collies are susceptible to a particular chemical in some flea treatments so we have to be very careful that these do not get an overdose or lick the pipette that is supposed to go on the skin.

Finally, we have the recreational drug toxicities. People are often worried about telling us that their dog may have eaten drugs as they think we will tell the police. Don't worry, we don't care what you want to do in your spare time, we just care about finding the right diagnosis for your pet as soon as possible so we know what to treat. For example, a six month old Staffordshire bull terrier came in one evening and was exhibiting very strange behaviour. He would lie down, stretch his front legs out in front of him, tilt his head back and howl for a few seconds. He'd then be able to get up, very wobbly and walk like a dressage pony with his front legs. I repeatedly asked if he could have got hold of any toxic substances in the house or garden like flea treatment or slug pellets. The owner told me that there was no way he could have had access to anything unusual so we started to make a plan for what I thought was a serious brain issue such as meningitis. Myself and the owner were very worried and we admitted him for investigation and treatment, with a view to referring him to a specialist in the morning. When I took him out the back to the nurses, they told me that one of them had been to school with the guy and he was known for smoking cannabis. I called him up and asked pointedly if Rocky could have had any access to cannabis, that we weren't going to report him but just needed to know as it simplified his treatment and would mean he wouldn't need any investigation. At this point, he admitted that he may have 'stolen some weed off the balcony as the neighbour likes the throw the ends of his joints onto it'. (Yeah, your 'neighbour', sure it was). Poor Rocky must have had quite the stash of it because he was the worst case of cannabis toxicity I'd ever seen; normally dogs are just falling over, wobbly and very disorientated.

After twelve hours on a drip, he was fine to go home again; knowing the cause had saved the owner hundreds of pounds and saved Rocky some blood tests and a trip to the neurologist. Often, you know from the smell of the person that the dog probably ate weed. Once, we had to apologise to a waiting room full of people for the smell in the room; we didn't want them thinking it was our staff having a particular happy lunch break. Luckily I've never seen anything more than this though I've had a neighbour bring in a guy with his dog once because he was so out of it that he couldn't drive; getting the pet's history out of him was a challenge. My friend who works at an emergency vets has seen a case of cocaine toxicity which sadly didn't go well for the dog due to overheating, but, and I quote,'at least he went out on a high.'

Rabbits aren't immune from the effects of toxicities even though they are often kept away from these things by being in a hutch. Sadly, I have seen a house rabbit become very poorly from chocolate toxicity as it stole some from beside the owner's bed and rabbits physiologically cannot be sick so we had to put it on a drip, give charcoal and hope for the best. Ironically, it was Easter time and it had eaten a chocolate bunny! Weird, cannibal rabbit! Guinea pigs cannot eat tomato plants - the fruit is fine but the leaves and stalk is poisonous. Again, they cannot vomit and putting them on a drip is near impossible. I saw a guinea pig out of hours who had eaten about 30cm of a tomato stalk and leaves which is rather a lot. We gave him some fluids under his skin and lots of drugs to make his guts keep moving and hopefully pass it through and thankfully, he was quite poorly but he did survive.

Toxicity cases can make us very happy because we can send home a healthy pet that we know full well would have died or become seriously ill without our intervention. A lot of the time they follow set protocols, meaning our job is that little bit easier. When we know what has been ingested, we can manage owner expectations from the start and get the pet on the right treatment as soon as possible.

As already discussed, it is pretty rare for us to know exactly what is causing a pet to be ill from the moment it comes into us. Sadly, a small percentage of the time these cases do not go the way we want them to, especially if they are presented further down the line because the owner didn't see them eat anything. However, this is the minority and we certainly won't let them go without a fight.

All veterinary staff would just recommend that you don't keep highly toxic substances in your home, such as lilies, slug pellets and anti-freeze. I have lost count of the number of lilies I have had to give to my neighbours or throw away because I have a cat. Anti-freeze sprays are much easier than scraping the ice off your car but please cope with the scraper to save your pets! Keep all drugs of any kind in a high cupboard that is inaccessible to pets and the same with any chocolate, grapes or raisins. Easter and Christmas are always busy times for us, and the fruit cake or hot cross bun cinnamon-y smell mingled with dog food vomit is something we like to avoid if possible.

REFERRAL CENTRES

Referral centres are big veterinary hospitals run by a team of specialist vets and nurses. Within the field of veterinary medicine, just like human medicine, there are a variety of specialisms to choose from. These include cardiology, oncology (cancer), orthopaedics, imaging, neurology, dermatology and ophthalmology. There are broader categories such as soft tissue surgery - vets who can do all the incredibly complicated operations that GP vets cannot perform; and small animal medicine - all the diseases of the abdominal organs and blood system. There are nurses that also do extra qualifications and courses in each of these areas that work alongside the vets. Not to mention all the other staff like physiotherapists, hydrotherapists and receptionists. If you have ever had to take your pet to a referral centre, you can see the incredible places that they are. State-of- the-art equipment such as MRI and CT scanners, plus better, costlier versions of all our normal investigative equipment such as ultrasound machines are found in pristine conditions. They have their own pathologists a lot of the time too - those that can look down microscopes and diagnose conditions based on biopsies, blood smears and sections of tumours. The dog and cat kennels are nice enough that you would want to stay in them yourself. There is a dedicated Intensive Care Unit with specialist vets and nurses in this area too, often giving your pet dedicated round-the-clock care.

Veterinary surgeons become specialists by many extra years of study after completing their normal university degree. A lot of specialists will have spent at least a year in a normal GP 'first opinion' practice but some do not as they know that they only want to specialise in a certain area to start with. The study starts with an internship at one of the referral hospitals which is a year of learning the basics of the specialism. In competitive situations, candidates will have to have completed more than one internship before being accepted into a 'residency'. This is a three or four year placement, working under a specialist in their certain field, learning everything that they need to know. Every scientific paper released in that subject for the last five years needs to be read and memorised plus everything from a multitude of textbooks. They know every obscure treatment and rare disease possible. At the end of this period of study, they have to pass notoriously difficult exams before they can call themselves a 'specialist'. Whilst studying, the intern and resident salaries are well below that of regular vets of the same level of experience as they are classed as 'students' as well as having a job. Luckily, once qualified as a specialist the salary finally rivals those of doctors and dentists, often reaching six digits by the end of their career. Given their level of knowledge and the extra years of study, this is very much deserved.

From the point of view of us GP vets, specialists can be incredible. Whenever we have a pet in who's illness we cannot diagnose, we will call a specialist for their help. If we take a set of x-rays and the images don't look like anything we have seen before, we can send these x-rays to an imaging specialist who can often give us an answer within a couple of hours if needed. Often we have to refer the pet to the referral centre for further tests and treatments that we cannot provide. Obviously, they will also know all the strange diseases that we have never seen. I have mentioned quite a few cases of this happening already, such as the cat with the odd ear condition and the puppy with the congenital diaphragmatic hernia. There are many more stories though!

There was a middle aged spaniel that I referred because it was very anaemic and looked like its immune system was destroying its own red blood cells, something that we see reasonably often in GP practice. However, she didn't seem to be responding to the normal treatment and the tests came back as negative for the condition we thought she had. The referral centre then found that she was indeed destroying her red blood cells, but before they were released into her blood stream at all! They were being made and then immediately destroyed in her own bone marrow. She recovered well with their treatment and I didn't feel bad at all for not being able to pick that one up.

Recently, I saw a cat who was scratching itself manically and causing multiple scabs around its face. This is something that is often associated with an allergy and normally responds to steroid injections. Milly didn't, so we took biopsies of the skin. This confirmed that she did have an allergy reaction so we ordered a different kind of drug to try. In the meantime, she then became very unwell and again, started to appear to destroy her own red blood cells. The specialist that I called for advice (who happened to be a good friend) suggested that she may have had a blood borne parasite that was allowed to proliferate because of the steroid treatment that dampens the immune system. I performed the tests and he was right! How he knew this just from looking at some history and blood tests is amazing.

This is why vets like specialists so much; it means we have someone to ask when we don't understand what is going on with a case and can send the pets to the referral centre so we don't have to spend all our time worrying about why we can't find the answer. I often wonder what they do when they don't know the answer. A recent case of a Doberman being kicked by a large deer answers that one for me. One of the major blood vessels to the heart became damaged in the process, something the specialist cardiologists had never seen before. So they asked the *human* cardiologists and together they formulated a surgical plan for her!

With all their fancy equipment, they can also treat and diagnose conditions that we wouldn't be able to, even when we know the theory behind it all. If we see a dog that has back pain and lacks reflexes in its back legs, we know that we should refer it for an MRI scan and spinal surgery. If a pet looks like it is having brain issues then we know we can't do too much to help it without an MRI and sample of the fluid from around the brain. If we diagnose a dog with a certain tumour that responds to radiotherapy, we have to refer it to a centre that has the correct machine. The same can be said for surgery. There are some orthopaedic operations that are too complicated for GP vets to perform so we have to send them to an orthopaedic specialist.

If a pet needs open chest surgery then it is much better off going to a place where they have anaesthetists that have dealt with that situation multiple times before and a surgeon who will have far more success than we would. Gall bladder, liver lobe and kidney removal are all things that have high complication rates even in the hands of these experienced surgeons and we are taught at university to send these to where they have the best surgical equipment and staff. If a cancer is in a very difficult place to remove and we know that it is likely to be malignant, referral to an oncologist to work out a surgical plan and chemotherapy is preferable. There are a whole array of congenital conditions that pets can get that require complex procedures to fix, such as liver shunts where the blood bypasses the liver and the toxins go around the bloodstream.

The brachycephalic dogs that require BOAS surgery have a very high post-op complication rate and this will be reduced as much as possible by going to a referral surgeon. In all these situations and many more, we will always offer referral to the best surgeons as that is the best thing for the animal. However, costs will very soon be in the thousands and can even reach £10,000 at some of these centres. Given the incredible work and care, this is often a fair price but without insurance, many people cannot afford it. In some situations, we will attempt surgery in the GP practice, knowing the pet will die without any intervention. We can also try to work off presumptive diagnoses, without any MRI or CT scanner to confirm out suspicions. This can all sometimes yield happy results but unfortunately, this is not always the way.

The only problem we do see with the referral centres is that they often involve a lot of big egos in one place. For the clients and the animals, this does not matter as they will receive fantastic care. Behind the scenes though, I know many stories of nurses and support staff being treated in very derogatory ways and expected to answer to the whims of the top specialists at the drop of a hat. Obviously, this is not always the way and I know a lot of lovely specialists too. However, it is not a pleasant situation for the other vets and nurses and something that is inexcusable to me.

Sending a very poorly pet off to a referral centre will often relieve the pressure on us GP vets. The reduction in stress and knowing the animal is in the best place is a blessing for us and allows us to be able to give our time and commitment to the next patient and client. If you ever get given the option to be referred to one of these clinics, know that it is the best thing for your pet and if finances allow, always go.

VACCINATIONS

We vets like vaccinations, or 'boosters', for a few reasons. Firstly and most importantly, due to the fact that they prevent some pretty nasty diseases. Secondly, because a vaccination appointment will often be a pleasant and speedy consult that allows us to catch up some time if we have overrun from more difficult consultations. Having a 'double booster' booked in, when there are two pets (or even more) from the same family is even better because we can do a thorough examination, chat to the owners about routine healthcare and give two vaccinations in the same amount of time as it takes to deal with one sick pet so suddenly we are back to running on time! We also do enjoy the fact that we can pick up on diseases early because if an animal is being brought in for its vaccination, they are usually fit and well so anything unusual we find is often in the early stages and thus can be treated more easily and carry a good prognosis. Heart murmurs are classic examples of this; any heart murmur picked up early and before clinical signs become apparent is much less serious to deal with than animals that haven't been seen for years and only come in when they have signs of coughing or exercise intolerance. Obviously, this is not always the case as a heart murmur could occur only a month after a booster appointment and it progresses over the next 11 months, but it is better than nothing! In recent years, there has been a rise in 'anti-vaccination' content over social media and the internet so there are a few pieces of information that I wanted to share with you about pet vaccines, all based *on my own experience.*

Dogs are routinely vaccinated against Distemper, Hepatitis from 'adenovirus', Parvovirus (the DHP vaccine) and leptospirosis. Distemper or 'hard pad disease' as it used to be called, was much more common a few decades ago before the vaccine became popular and is rarely seen in the UK now though is more common abroad. One of the older vets that I used to work with who retired recently can still remember seeing quite a few cases when he was younger. There are many symptoms associated with it, from diarrhoea and respiratory signs to skin sores and thickening of the pads. In some cases, neurological symptoms such as seizures or tremors can occur too and it can present similar to rabies. Treatment can be successful in a few cases but if left too long, pneumonia can cause death and those that have neurological signs will not often improve.

Parvovirus causes bloody vomiting and diarrhoea; animals are very lethargic and in pain with gut cramps; it is often fatal even with days of intensive treatment. Adenovirus causes a particular type of hepatitis (liver failure) and will cause lethargy, vomiting, abdominal pain and not eating; again it requires days of hospitalisation and doesn't have a good prognosis. All these viruses are transferred by other dogs leaving excretions in the environment. Leptospira are odd organisms that are a bit like a cross between a bacteria and a worm; they cause leptospirosis which causes liver and kidney failure and is passed in urine of infected dogs and rats. It can also pass to humans.

Cats are vaccinated against cat flu, leukaemia (FeLV) and panleucopenia. Cat flu is caused by a mixture of different viruses and bacteria, with the vaccine protecting against calicivirus and herpesvirus-1. It is passed from cat to cat in a similar way to colds in humans and even if cats are not showing clinical signs, they can still pass it to cats that have no immunity such as from the mother cat to kittens. This causes recurrent respiratory signs throughout the cat's life, sometimes with inflamed gums too which can be painful. They get conjunctivitis and eye ulcers and can generally feel unwell for a few days though in older or very young cats, it can lead to pneumonia and death.

Panleucopenia is similar to parvovirus in dogs but can also cause destruction of the bone marrow and brain damage in kittens that are infected whilst in the womb. It is also passed via secretions from other cats. Feline leukaemia virus (FeLV) causes immunosuppression and makes cats more vulnerable to overwhelming infections that can cause them to become very unwell and even die from infections that would not be serious in healthy cats. It also predisposes them to many types of cancer including leukaemia itself. It is passed from bites from other cats so is not needed in indoor cats whereas the other viruses can be brought in on your hands and clothes.

There are various vaccine protocols throughout the UK and worldwide but most practices will follow certain guidelines. The timings of the puppy and kitten vaccines are so that their own immunity is then at a good level when the maternal antibodies wane at around twelve weeks of age. The World Small Animal Veterinary Association (WSAVA) vaccination guidelines actually recommend four vaccines in the first six months of a puppy's life to 'guarantee 'immune response. Vet practices will only routinely do two sets of vaccines, 2-4 weeks apart, due to concern of over-vaccinating, costs, compliance and not having to inflict a needle on them too often! The leptospirosis protection depends on whether the L4 or L2 vaccine is used (L2 protects against two strains, L4 against four); both can be given alongside the DHP any time from eight weeks of age. The second L2 can be given with the second DHP after two weeks but the second L4 can only be given after four weeks which will delay the puppy being allowed out for walks and socialising. This problem isn't so bad for cats who shouldn't be allowed out until they have been neutered anyway but their vaccines tend to start at nine weeks of age and are two injections, 3-4 weeks apart. After their initial course of vaccination, the first year booster is very important to top up the immunity and the full vaccine is given again at this point. After this, we give DHP every three years to dog, and L2 or L4 every year. For cats, we give cat flu every year, FeLV every three years and panleucopenia every year or three years depending on the brand but it is only really needed every three years.

Titre testing can be performed for those vaccines that cause an antibody response that can be accurately measured. This is the case for the DHP vaccine in dogs, but only for panleucopenia in cats. I have performed quite a few of these titre tests and it is common for the DHP results to come back with a good immunity against one of the three diseases still but not for the other two. There is a separate parvovirus vaccine if this is the one that falls below the appropriate antibody levels but there isn't a vaccine for just the distemper or hepatitis parts which is both frustrating and makes the testing slightly obsolete in a few cases. Some dogs will have an immune response that means that each time we do these tests, usually yearly, their antibody levels are always above the threshold for at least one of them and this can be for years and years. In others, the antibody response falls quite rapidly and the vaccines have to be done according to the normal protocols or even earlier. There is no way of telling from the outside which dog will do which! We are always happy to perform an antibody titre test but a leptospirosis vaccine should be given yearly anyway as there is no way to test for the immunity levels for this. In cats, there is a separate vaccine that doesn't include the panleucopenia part so titres can be done for this but the cat flu vaccine has to be given yearly. Titre testing can be quite expensive but it is probably the best way of ensuring your dog's immunity is kept up to date if you do have fears of giving the vaccines.

The majority of the public will vaccinate their dogs, at least as puppies. Cats are less routinely vaccinated but I would say that over half of them at least get their kitten vaccines. Now let's do some maths to work out the risks of vaccine reactions. I would say that on average, I vaccinate six or seven pets per day which adds up to over a two thousand per year. I have been a vet for over seven years, so that is fourteen thousand vaccines I have given. There are about ten vets at my old practice so let's say we have done 140,000 vaccines over the time I have been there. I have seen a handful of minor reactions that the owners have either called us about or brought their pet in to see us for. These have been due to minor swellings on the face or at the vaccine site, a couple of days of vomiting and diarrhoea or general lethargy. For future vaccinations, these pets would have titre tests to check for immunity levels, have a different brand of vaccine, or anti-histamines before vaccinations. Some owners were happy once the pet recovered and just knew they'd be unwell for a couple of days post vaccine.

Very sadly, my old colleague has seen one cat who has had an injection site cancer form in the place of the vaccination. This required radical surgery to remove but the cat succumbed to the cancer and had to be put down. Injection site cancers can occur from the result of any injection of any substance, not just vaccines, and are exceedingly rare. We recently had one dog become very unwell and sadly die as a direct result of a vaccination. It was a puppy who had an auto-immune reaction and went into multi-organ failure. We can't prove it was related to the vaccine but we have a pretty strong suspicion, as does the referral centre. This is absolutely tragic and I can understand the owners of both these pets never wanting to vaccinate a pet again.

However, also in my career, we have seen about thirty cases of confirmed parvovirus, including one set of five Labrador puppies from an unvaccinated mother. Over half of these dogs died or were put to sleep, including most of those puppies over the course of a few days. The others only survived after days of intensive hospitalisation. We have seen five confirmed cases of leptospirosis (plus some more suspected) and one of adenovirus.

Most of these were put to sleep or died, the others going home after several days of drips, drugs, feeding tubes and intensive care. I cannot even begin to count the number of cases of cat flu we have seen as it is in the hundreds and probably pushing towards a thousand. The majority of these cats have multiple flare ups a year of weepy eyes, nose, sneezing and lethargy rather like a human cold or conjunctivitis. This is obviously not pleasant but not terrible, though it becomes costly over time. Sometimes, it can then lead to inappetence and lung infections depending on the severity. Sadly, some very badly affected kittens have had to have eyes removed due to deep ulcerations and some old cats have had to be put to sleep due to terrible pneumonias. I have also seen about twenty cases of FeLV, either picked up on stray cats or tested for after a cat becomes very unwell. Luckily, I have only seen one case of panleucopenia that was an 'in utero 'infection and the kitten was happy, just walked around lifting up its front legs like it was walking on something cold for all of its life!

When presented with these figures, you can see why my own opinion is that the risk of a bad vaccination reaction is much lower than that of becoming very poorly from the actual disease. Vaccination is never 100% effective and animals can still get these diseases because of a failure of immune reaction or a different or new strain that there isn't a vaccine against. Every case of the diseases I have seen have been in unvaccinated animals apart from seven of the parvovirus cases that were due to a new strain in the area.

Many people who argue against vaccination will use side effects as one argument but another is that the risk of getting the disease is very low compared to the size of the population of pets. What these people seem to forget is that the cases are low *because* of vaccination. There are records of distemper cases in just one London clinic in the nineteenth century that had over two hundred cases in one year whereas only five cases have been reported across the whole of the UK in the last seven years.

The risk of your pets developing these horrible diseases is much lower now but if everyone stopped vaccinating, the cases would rise again and the risk to your pet would be much greater. Just look at the recent measles outbreak in the USA. Leptospirosis is the trickiest of organisms to vaccinate against as there is no sure way to determine how long immunity lasts for, with some studies suggesting that it is under a year and more like six months. We therefore give the vaccine yearly rather than every three years like the DHP vaccine. This may not actually be enough but it is a compromise that we think makes the most sense. The headlines such as 'L4 vaccine killed my dog' would make anyone sit and think about whether to give the vaccine and I will respect a decision to give the L2 vaccine instead. None of the deaths have been proven to be linked to the vaccine though and personally, I have not seen any reactions to the many hundreds of L4 vaccines I have given in my time as a locum. A few cases of leptospirosis in the UK each year are attributed to those two extra strains that the L4 protects against, so there is a small risk associated with the L2 vaccine in not covering for these.

Rabbits also require vaccinations yearly, though they don't tend to need the primary course that dogs and cats do, just a one-off injection to start. They are vaccinated against myxomatosis, something that you may have seen in wild rabbits if you've ever been unlucky to come across a dead one. They get inflamed, ulcerated eyes and faces, with respiratory issues that lead to death in the majority of cases. This is transmitted by any blood sucking insect such as fleas, mites, ticks and mosquitoes. Rabbits are also vaccinated against Rabbit Haemorrhagic Disease type 1 and 2, the most common symptom of these being sudden death though sometimes bleeding from the eyes, nose and bruising can be seen. Yes, 'sudden death' is a symptom in this disease; one minute you're hopping along and then the next, you're dead. Pretty tricky to treat that one. It is spread between rabbits via bodily fluids. RHD 2 wasn't seen in the UK until a few years ago when we started seeing sudden deaths in the wild and domestic rabbits. The vaccinations that have been produced since then have dramatically reduced the number of deaths that we have seen.

I have seen just one reaction to a rabbit vaccine with skin sores appearing all over the body. These resolved and the rabbit has been happy since. Any outdoor rabbit should be vaccinated against all three diseases. Just like with indoor cats, the risk of indoor bunnies catching the diseases is minute so we understand not vaccinating but we still do recommend it just in case you bring anything in on your hands and clothes.

You see there are always arguments for and against anything in life and it is difficult to know what to do for the best. How do you know that the anti-vaccine reports of their dog dying post vaccine are true or whether it is completely unrelated? How do you know that the vaccine company studies into the side effects aren't skewed towards a pro-vaccine message? You don't. That is why I am just telling you everything from *my own experience only*. I have far more opinions about pet vaccines outside the scope of this chapter but there is no point in my quoting things that I have not been directly involved in because I cannot personally verify the studies so it is not going to persuade anyone otherwise. For those people that do have fears of vaccinations, the likelihood of your pets contracting any illnesses that can be prevented by vaccination is still very low and the majority of the time, anyone who doesn't vaccinate their pets will benefit from the herd immunity brought about by those of us that do. However, the risk of getting these illnesses is still much higher than the risk of any vaccination reaction, in my own experience. The risk of death from these illnesses is certainly much, much higher. At the very least, give the course as a puppy or kitten, plus the booster after a year. This will hopefully give immunity for the first few years of life and possibly more beyond, depending on the individual animal's immune system. If you can afford to titre test your dog then this is even better. Although we vets like a booster appointment for the fact that it is usually a nice occasion where we can chat to owners without any worry over the pet's illness and that we can catch up any lost time, we mainly like giving the vaccinations in the knowledge that we are doing what we believe is the best and right thing for the pet.

LAUGHING AT SILLY THINGS WE READ ONLINE

Vets often have people come to see them for advice and remark that they 'read on that internet that such and such is true'. The majority of these statements are about certain possible diagnoses, treatments that were recommended or the dangers of certain products. Some of them are so very random and out there that they stick in your mind. In all these situations, we have to remain as professional as possible and not laugh or express our own opinions too fiercely. However, we do then like to go to the other staff members and do a quick internet search ourselves to see what else we can find. There have been countless occasions like this but these are the most hilarious and the most common ones.

A recently rehomed male dog was brought into see me because of some lumps on his abdomen. He was a new dog owner so very conscientious. The owners had read online that they could be cancerous lumps, especially give there were many of them and was very worried. I couldn't find any lumps on its abdomen and looked quizzically at the owner. I asked him to show me the lumps that he had found. He then pointed at a few little lumps all down both sides of the dog's abdomen so I told him that they were, in fact, his nipples. The man looked at me incredulously and exclaimed that his dog was male and had a penis so how could he have nipples too? I then asked him if had both a penis and nipples and he laughed at his own silliness. We often have people bringing in animals that have ticks that they can't remove and they sometimes turn out to be nipples, skin tags or warts. Imagine someone trying to pull off your nipple! I have had a couple of owners bring in their female dogs, telling me they are male and pointing at their 'penis 'which is actually their vulva. We cannot always criticise this though as young cats and rabbits are very difficult to sex. My colleague has seen a dog who was a hermaphrodite - they had a small penis growing out of their vulva!

There was a time that a man brought in his dog that was having a seizure. He had done a quick internet search as to what he could do in this situation and was told that putting chamomile tea up its bottom would help bring him out of the seizure. Given we are told that chamomile tea is good for relaxing us, he believed this and made some. I didn't ask how he got it up the dog's bottom and needless to say, it didn't help. He then made the wise decision to bring it into see us, we gave it some rectal diazepam and the fitting stopped. This is not the only time I have had people try to give medication as a suppository. An owner gave their dog the oral probiotic and kaolin paste we dispensed for its diarrhoea up its bottom, though I can at least see the logic there. I recently had a consultation where I happened to empty the dog's anal glands at the same time as giving it some medication for its ongoing skin disease. The owner got very confused and thought that she was meant to give the medication up his bottom to help his anal glands.

We always get a lot of questions in the summer about how to cool pets down in the hotter weather. One of the things we suggest is to put ice cubes in their water. Dogs will often just play with ice cubes anyway which can help. My colleague was then told by an owner that she had read on social media that this is actually very bad for them and makes them warmer. Very confused, we had a quick look at the article and read that swallowing the ice cold water, or chips from the ice cube, makes the receptors at the back of the throat think that they are actually too cold and brings about changes to warm them up. This is absolutely not true! Giving them ice cubes will definitely help cool them down.

An owner came in to see my colleague once because her dog had diarrhoea. She had read on the internet to feed some chicken to settle its diarrhoea and was furious that this hadn't helped. It can be good advice to suggest chicken but what the internet failed to say was 'plain chicken', or 'bland'. The owner had fed it a bucket of Kentucky fried chicken and wondered why this had made the diarrhoea worse.

On the subject of food, the internet likes to fuel the ongoing discussions over which is the best diet to feed your pet. Over the last few years, grain free diets have become more fashionable due to the thought that some of the allergies that we see in pets are due to the grains. We certainly do see the occasional allergy to these grains or various other carbohydrates when we test for allergens. However, a lot of websites will try to claim that this is the only thing in the food that pets can be allergic to. This is definitely not true and we see a large amount of animals who are allergic to protein sources too, one of the most common being chicken. Quite a lot of the foods out there are grain free now so a reasonable proportion of our pets are on them. Most of the time, this is completely unnecessary in most dogs as grains contain quite a few essential vitamins and minerals. There is now a trend between dogs being fed a grain free diet and a certain heart disease called dilated cardiomyopathy. This can be fatal within a few months and tends to be seen in large breed dogs. Some atypical breeds are now developing this condition and it is thought that this may be due to the grain free diets. This hypothesis has been supported by the fact that the heart returns to normal when the diet is changed to one containing grains. There is no clear reason as to why this is the case yet and it needs more research but it is something to keep in mind.

The other diet that gets a lot of attention is the raw diet - usually a mix of raw meats and ground up bone, with some encouraging whole bones to be eaten too. These are often frozen and then need to be defrosted daily. Again, this can have a lot of advantages if there is a medical need. Those pets with allergies to certain food substances, or storage mites that can be found in bags of dog kibble, will improve on this type of food if the right ingredients are picked. They produce smaller amounts of faeces and the food can help with chronic diarrhoea. Although I think that a large majority of those animals that are raw fed never see any problems, we vets tend to see the ones that do thus we have a prejudice against them. I've seen a dog who had a stricture that formed in its colon due to the impaction of the ground up bones. This meant that he couldn't defaecate properly and had to keep having procedures to remove large amount of faeces. Eventually, his quality of life suffered so much that the owner decided to put him to sleep and he was only middle-aged. We have seen a few cases of bones perforating the oesophagus or guts, especially when silly dogs try to swallow the whole bone and it gets stuck. Then there are the countless cases of salmonella and campylobacter food poisoning that we see in cats and dogs fed raw chicken. Animals that chew on bones a lot tend to have cleaner teeth but they also have a higher incidence of tooth fractures. When you see all of these issues, it is easy to wonder why you would run the risk of giving the raw diets.

On top of all this, you have the human health implications from the residues left in the food bowls and in the pet's mouth when they lick you. There is very recent evidence out there that many multi-drug resistant bacteria are found in households where pets are fed raw food, another massive concern for pet and human healthcare. We often giggle when people tell us they want their dog to be raw fed because 'it is similar to a wolf which is more natural and like in the wild'. Since when does your pug look like a wolf? I'd like to see a pack of pugs trying to bring down a deer or catch a pheasant (please take a moment to visualise that image). The gut bacteria found in domestic dogs are now so different from the population found in the guts of wolves that they are actually more similar to human gut bacteria. Would you eat raw chicken? I hope not. Well, you are doing if you let you raw-fed dog lick your face. If you really do want to raw feed, please stick to the beef, lamb or venison and steer clear of the poultry and pork.

Some things we see online don't make us laugh but make us very concerned instead. This is mainly due to vaccinations as already mentioned. The other major concern is parasite treatment, sometimes due to the possible side effects but also due to the environmental impact these chemicals are causing. There is new evidence to suggest that the chemicals in collars and spot-on products are being found in the waterways and having an impact on the insect population and therefore the birds and other predators too. This is due to those parasitic treatments used in large animals as well as our pets. For a lot of vets, this is very concerning and not something that I want to be happening as a result of products that I prescribe. I tried not to give my cat preventative flea treatment at first and thought I'd just treat her if they occurred but after she got fleas twice in a few months, I now do treat her monthly and spray my house once a year. She is also an avid hunter so has had worms too; it crawled out of her bum and onto my friend's lap. I promptly treated her and use the products every few months or so.

The problem is that most products that have reduced concentration of chemicals in, such as those bought in supermarkets or pet shops, don't actually work. We have had a lot of animals brought into us with frustrated owners who have spent a lot of money in the pet shops or on natural products and can't get rid of fleas. The only products that work are the stronger chemicals. There are oral products available instead but there is a possibility that some of the chemicals are still excreted in the urine or faeces. These oral products tend to be the ones that are bad-mouthed online due to their 'terrible side effects'. We see minor side effects to certain flea and worming treatments reasonably commonly, such as vomiting or localised skin reactions. In these cases, we suggest not using that product again and switching to another.

There are so many products available, especially as fleas have mutated against some of the older products and there is not one product that effectively treats against everything. There are a few reports of more serious adverse events occurring after certain products but a lot of these are events that have happened many days to weeks after the taking of the product so it is difficult to know if they are related. Certainly, most toxins that we know of in veterinary medicine will show their effects within three or four days of ingestion, the majority starting within twelve hours. All I can say is that personally, I have never seen anything more than a minor reaction to a *veterinary prescribed* parasite treatment.

Avoiding using blanket parasite treatment has a lot of argument behind it. It is actively encouraged in the equine world to do faecal egg counts rather than blanket worm treatment and there are services out there that provide this option for dogs and cats too but they are cost prohibitive a lot of the time. It would be great if there were cheaper ways of doing this in the future. It is very easy to test for fleas - get yourself a flea comb or simply hold your pet over some wet white paper or tissue and rub vigorously. Flea dirt will fall off and show as little black dots that dissolve into a red patch on the wet, white paper as it is digested blood. If you see this, get a flea product from us. Running your hands over all their skin every 24 hours in the summer months will pick up most ticks and you can remove them with a tick remover. If this occurs a lot, then maybe a tick repellant will be a good idea. Look out for worms and worm segments in faeces in dogs; if your cat defaecates outside and hunts a lot then maybe using a product every few months is good and if they start to lose weight, definitely treat them then.

We are taught all the terrible diseases that can occur in both humans and animals if parasites are not prevented and this is why vets prescribe these products. Certain worms can cause blindness in children; fleas can initiate allergies in some cats and rarely can transmit some blood parasites like mycoplasma; ticks can carry Lyme's disease to people as well as pets and are a source of many other blood parasites; lungworm in slugs and snails causes coughing, can stop blood clotting and causes many deaths per year, sometimes suddenly; when this is what you know, do you blame us for not wanting your pets or you to be put at risk? Tick-borne diseases are very rare in the UK, but in other countries stopping your pet getting tick bites and tick-borne fever is extremely important. If you have young children then using worming treatment in your pets is a good idea. When in hot countries where sandflies are present, it is paramount to use repellant collars to stop your pet getting Leishmania from the sandflies, something we see more and more of in imported rescue dogs. If your dog eats slugs and snails, giving prevention for lungworm is probably worth the risk of any medications. It is all about weighing up the risks and benefits in each case. If you don't want to use certain products, we can provide alternatives if you want to use prevention. If you don't want to use any prevention at all and just use treatment if parasites are found, this is also absolutely fine and is something that the veterinary profession will likely move towards as the environmental impact comes to the forefront of all our lives.

The other big topic that gives us a bit of a giggle is homeopathy (you could see this one coming, right?) And no, I'm not about to slate anything that's not a drug; I have tried to keep an open mind during the research for this chapter. Some of it did make me actually bark with laughter though..

Firstly, there is a difference between homeopathy and nutraceuticals. Nutraceuticals are those things that aren't manufactured drugs but are 'supplements', usually naturally occurring products or slight modifications of them that are then added to or found naturally in food. Joint supplements such as omega 3 and 6 essential fatty acids, green lipped mussel extract, glucosamine, *Boswellia* plant extract and turmeric have evidence for their use in slowing down the progression of arthritis, lubrication of the joints and a mild pain killing and anti-inflammatory effect. Skin supplements such as vitamin A, E anti-oxidants and biotin can certainly help maintain the natural skin barrier. Milk thistle extract is definitely good for the liver. Probiotics and prebiotics have evidence to suggest that they can help with both acute and chronic diarrhoea in pets. The gut flora is a fascinating area of research, thought to interfere with the function of the skin and brain too. Some evidence exists for the use of cranberry juice extract, N-acetyl D-glucosamine or D-mannose in bladder inflammation and infection. Certainly, anti-stress ingredients such as L-tryptophan in bladder supplements and pheromone plug ins can make a huge difference to stress cystitis in cats. There is evidence that Vitamin B and E, Ginkgo plant extract and certain amino acids can help brain function in dementia patients.

Nutraceuticals don't have any regulation and do not need to go through any form of clinical trial to be advertised whereas pharmaceutical drugs do. Many pharmaceutical drugs started life as a nutraceutical or as 'traditional medicine'. For example, aspirin comes from willow leaves and bark, atropine from the foxglove plant, opium from poppies. Pharmaceutical drugs tend to be a purified form of the extracts from these plants, or a synthetic version grown in a lab. The NSAID class of drugs like ibuprofen in humans and meloxicam in dogs all derive from the aspirin in willow. A lot of antibiotics come from soil-dwelling organisms and their derivatives. Most people know the story of the birth of penicillin, just from Fleming accidentally leaving some agar plates to go mouldy.

True homeopathic products differ from nutraceuticals, though many homeopathic vets are happy for nutraceuticals to be used too. The general principle of homeopathy is to give a dilution of an active ingredient into the body in some way. Usually, this is based on the 'like-cures-like 'process, assuming that something that causes the signs in a pet's body will also cure those same signs if given to them when they are poorly with them. At each stage of dilution of the active ingredient, the remedy is shaken or disturbed in some way as this is thought to increase the potency of the ingredient and add energy. For example, cutting an onion causes your nose and eyes to run and so it is thought that it may help to cause decongestion from the signs of a cold. However, it is apparently not the cutting, or eating, of an onion that will cure the signs of a cold. Taking the active ingredient *Allium cepa* and successively diluting it, shaking it to inject vital energy and increase potency to create the homeopathic treatment - this will help alleviate signs of a cold. Ironically, this is a reasonably similar principle to the making of a vaccination - injecting a weakened, dead or diluted version of the actual pathogen that causes the disease. Sadly, homeopathic vaccinations that are taken orally have active ingredients that are no longer detectable because they have been diluted too many times and have not shown any effectiveness in clinical trials.

Although I can see the principle behind some of these homeopathic remedies, some of the things that we read online actually cause us to burst out laughing or crying from sadness for the poor pet. One sight sells eye drops made from fennel to cure glaucoma and writes that 'a blind dog can still be a happy dog '- true but glaucoma is incredibly painful and regardless of whether a dog is blind, it is still cruel to leave them in pain. I read that 'all skin disease is related to liver function 'so giving liver support will cure the thousands of dogs with allergic skin disease apparently. You can get homeopathic remedies from your dog made from the *light of Venus*. Not sure which clinical signs the light of Venus causes and thus treats and I can't seem to find the answer anywhere. This obviously led me to a rabbit-hole of hilarious homeopathic remedies. The majority of the time, I cannot actually find a mechanism of action for the remedy or their theory as to what symptoms it causes and therefore treats. In those that I could, these are my personal favourites; the remedy made from fragments of a shipwreck on a beach in Wales to cure the feeling of 'stuckness 'in commuters getting stuck in traffic jams; the Berlin Wall remedy to reduce the feelings of being separated and isolated; the same feelings of disconnection and separation could also be helped by using the latex remedy, *made from a condom*. It is worth noting that latex is also good at helping any work related problems because 'rubber and going to work are strongly linked 'due to all the tyres out there, taking people on their commute.

Personally, despite my scepticism, I have no problem with people trialling homeopathic remedies first for minor conditions or even chronic, end-stage problems. The fewer chemicals we put into the waterways, the better. Avoiding unnecessary antibiotic use is something every vet is keen for and I would prefer an owner to trial any other remedies rather than just coming in demanding antibiotics when it is not needed. Certain skin conditions will undoubtedly improve with any cream application and by stopping the pet licking. When we have taken blood tests and the area looks bruised, we have a tube of Arnica cream to apply so using it at home for any skin lesions is a good starting point. Many viruses usually have to pass themselves and though we can provide supportive care to help an animal feel better sooner, the body will do its own job unless there are underlying immune conditions. Olbas oil steaming will certainly help any nasal congestion issues and is something we do in the hospital too!

Diarrhoea will often improve without the use of any drugs, just with time and a change to a bland diet. If your cat has end-stage kidney disease, certain tonics prescribed by homeopaths are unlikely to do any harm given water is good for kidney disease, and even pharmaceutical drugs can only do so much in these situations. Diets prescribed by homeopaths for certain conditions can often mimic those made by food manufacturer companies. Therefore, so long as you do your research to make sure the diet contains all the amino acids and minerals a pet needs, such as taurine in cats, I have no problem with this either. For an owner to refuse chemotherapy for their pet is completely understandable as it is a lot to put an animal through when they don't know why it is happening. I am on board with any homeopathic remedies for cancers in the hope that they may make a difference, so long as when you can see your pet is suffering, you still make the decision to let them go.

Aside from traditional homeopathic remedies, most vets are very keen for the use of nutraceuticals so if you do not want any pharmaceutical drugs, these are a good option to try. Not a day goes by without me suggesting some kind of supplement and I use them for my cat and for myself. Ironically, despite their evidence for use and the fact that a lot of the time I am recommending things bought online and not through the vet practice so not making us any money, a lot of people look at me like I'm trying to pull the wool over their eyes. These nutraceuticals really can make a great difference but people think anything 'natural 'will not work. So here we are as vets fighting both sides of the battle! Some people only want natural remedies, others think they are all useless.

With homeopathy, my issues come (as with a lot of people) when animals are suffering because owners refuse to use conventional drugs for pain relief or other forms of discomfort. For example, a dog that is itching itself uncontrollably that does not improve with homeopathic treatment, skin supplements and a diet change should then be given the opportunity for an itch-free life with pharmaceutical drugs. A cat that has been bitten by another cat, has had the abscess flushed and lanced, trialled homeopathy and is now becoming systemically unwell due to the infection and pain, should be given antibiotics and prefer-ably some pain relief too. If you want to use diatomaceous earth or low concentration garlic powder as flea and worm prevention then please do but use a veterinary licensed product if they do actually still get parasites. A pet that is limping due to arthritis and hasn't improved much on joint supplements, turmeric and homeopathic pain relief, should be given the chance to live an-other happy few months to years with pharmaceutical pain re-lief. If you truly don't believe in the use of modern medicine then you should be prepared to accept that your pet is still suffering, whatever the cause is, and put them to sleep when necessary.

There is also the concern over the welfare of the many animals that are actually used as *part of* alternative remedies. I'm sure most people have heard about the bears that are caged and have their bile extracted from the gall bladder or the poaching of ele-phants for their ivory to be used in traditional Chinese medicine. Please also be aware that traditional Chinese medicine products are not homeopathy as they are not diluted and don't use the same theories behind them. Some of these products contain toxic levels of heavy metals such as arsenic and lead and should be avoided in people, let alone animals.

We hope that the use of cannabidiol (CBD) oil products will be a good compromise in the future though more studies need to be done to find out a dose range for lots of treatments. The CBD oil works in a similar way to the drug gapabentin so is good for neuropathic pain. The studies performed so far have concluded dose ranges from 1-2mg/kg show effective pain relief perceived by both owners and vets, which can become quite costly. Some dogs require doses as low as 0.3mg/kg to show pain killing effects but a lot of products give doses that are much smaller.

This makes us concerned that owners will use these low doses and think that their pets are pain-free when this is very much not the case. At the higher doses of 2mg/kg, liver parameters showed an increase over the study period so it may not be without its side effects, we just don't know for sure yet. I am more than happy for anyone to trial CBD oil as pain relief, or for seizure and anxiety management and let me know their thoughts the next time I see them as it would be great for us to have another product to add to our list of things to use, especially one that is deemed more natural.

One of the things that gave us one of the biggest laughs recently was when a client told us she was paying to have distance reiki performed on her pet. For those of you who don't know, reiki is healing through the transfer of energy from one life source to another by holding your hands over the area of concern. This energy is similar to that transferred or absorbed by crystals when using another pseudoscience called 'crystal healing'. This energy force is something that has been believed for centuries and although no scientific evidence ever proves that it exists and that the healing practices work, it is certainly not going to do any harm to try these things. However, if a reiki healer has to transfer energy from one living thing to another, how on earth can that energy be transferred from their hands to your pet *via a photograph*? Yes, this happened during the pandemic. Some reiki healer was asking their clients to send in photos of the pets so she could heal them 'from a distance'. It is baffling to us that someone would pay £50 per session for such a thing quite happily, yet complain about the price of our services. We understand that it is through sheer desperation that someone would try anything when all else is failing and it is rather sad that there are people taking advantage of this situation. Maybe they do truly believe that 'distance reiki' will work for people's pets and they are not exploiting people but this seems very misguided to me. An owner that I met recently had trained herself in reiki and was convinced that her dog's fatty lumps were getting smaller so maybe I am being cynical in not believ-ing in the art of reiki at all.

Other types of alternative medicine are practices such as acu-puncture and chiropractic manipulation. Acupuncture is the insertion of needles into specific points to help stimulate the central nervous system and release neurotransmitters and hor-mones to bring about relaxation and the body's own heal-ing. Chiropractic healing aims to treat vertebral subluxations, putting less pressure on the nerves and releasing energy. The scientific evidence behind these is fairly inconclusive with some studies showing fair results, others showing that it doesn't help at all. I have had one dog with spinal pain that went to an acupuncturist and this did seem to help a lot; one of the nurses where I have been a locum takes her cat to acupuncture often. Some clients swear by their dog's chiropractor or massage ther-apist, though it is hard to tell if it is actually the pain relief and joint supplements that are helping. We know that physiotherapy and hydrotherapy are wonderful and can make a vast improve-ment to various orthopaedic and muscular issues. Laser therapy is a newer form of complementary therapy that is showing some promising results too.

As a final point, there are many 'old wives tales 'out there that are also not true. Pets having a cold, wet nose is not a sign of health. I have genuinely had appointments booked in for having a 'hot, dry nose'. Ok, maybe reception need some training on this one too. I have seen many animals on the brink of death with cold, wet noses. It means absolutely nothing and we are not sure where it came from! Also, a pet licking at something is most certainly *not* cleaning it. Their mouths are full of bac-teria even when they have healthy teeth so it is likely to cause an infection and the constant abrasion from their tongue makes matters worse. Oh and if someone writes that a limping pet isn't in pain, they are wrong. When you stand on something or twist your ankle, you then limp on that leg don't you? Why? Because it hurts to put pressure through it. So when an old dog is limping on an arthritic leg or if a cat isn't putting on of its legs on the floor, even if they aren't crying out, they are still in pain.

So in a very simple conclusion - please do not believe most of what you read on the internet; some of it may be true but please ask your vet. Your *vet*, by the way. Not your breeder. Or groomer. Or the person who owned a dog 25 years ago and talks about how much simpler pet health care seemed to be then. They didn't give pain relief for operations 25 years ago in animal medicine, do you really want to go back there?

CAESARIANS

Caesarians, or C-sections, are operations that we perform on a semi-regular basis to remove puppies or kittens directly from the uterus of the mother whilst she is under anaesthetic. This is normally as a result of difficulty giving birth. The large majority of female cats (called 'queens') and most breeds of dog will whelp (give birth) naturally with no problem. They've done it for hundreds of years without human intervention. Sadly, mainly due to said human intervention, there are a few breeds of dog now that struggle to pass puppies *most* of the time. This is the case for a large percentage of bulldogs; most commonly the French bulldogs but also British bulldogs. Most of this is due to the constant breeding for 'desirable 'characteristics that, over time, has led to their heads being too big to pass through the narrow pelvic canal. Ridiculous, isn't it? Let's breed some dogs that wouldn't be able to even be born without surgical intervention (cue eye roll). There are some bulldogs that do pass litters naturally and we like these ones, especially if they also have longer snouts and wider nostrils! Any breed of dog or cat can give the occasional overly large foetus that can get stuck in a similar way too.

Animals tend to start the process of labour with some restlessness, panting and pacing. They will often find a place to hide away to give birth, especially cats, so that they are safely away from predators whilst they are vulnerable. Of course, they like to whelp at night too so that they are less likely to be seen, something that is much to the dismay of the breeders and the vets that have to deal with the issues.

After a couple of hours of constant pushing, if nothing is coming out, any bitch or queen in labour will need to be seen by a vet. At this point, we can assess the animal, have a feel to see if any pups or kittens are stuck and try to help her out with some oxytocin injections to stimulate more contractions. I once had to see an elderly Labrador that had been mated accidentally (no, dogs do not go through the menopause) and was just too exhausted to go through labour herself. We gave her oxytocin and some calcium as this can often become low during labour. I gave her a one-off dose of an anti-inflammatory painkiller but we cannot give anything stronger than this whilst the puppies are alive in the abdomen and a dog isn't going to inhale gas and air! They also would never stay still for us to perform an epidural whilst conscious. Next, with my dainty little fingers, I could help mum deliver each of the puppies. Sadly, a few of them were stillborn, likely due to her age and the length of time she had been in labour before being brought in, but at least she didn't have to go through surgery.

If we think that either the babies or the mum is in danger, we will take them to surgery right away. In normal hours, we have a vet performing the surgery whilst a nurse monitors the anaesthetic closely. We then have two or three other nurses/vets/vet students to start reviving the puppies or kittens. As you can imagine, the surgery isn't the most straightforward of procedures because you are trying to get all the babies out as quickly as possible before the anaesthetic sinks into their own blood stream and causes them to become too drowsy to wake up and breathe. We are also trying to get all of the bodies out of one incision in the uterus so that there isn't more than one incision at risk of breaking down or causing adhesions to complicate further litters.

The anaesthetic is a bit more dodgy than a normal anaesthetic due to the pressure on the lungs and the major blood vessels from the multitude of puppies or kittens in the abdomen. There can be a massive drop in blood pressure and we don't have many options for drugs that don't pass into the milk. Whilst one nurse is looking after the mum, the other vet staff are reviving the babies. Usually, the act of coming through the narrow pelvic canal pushes the fluid out of the lungs of the puppy or kitten and stimulates it to breathe. With C-sections, we carefully remove the puppies from the uterus, still in the amniotic sac and pass it to the nurse without touching her and contaminating our surgical hands with bacteria. She then has to rip off the sac, clear the fluid from the nose and mouth, cut the cord then rub the puppy frantically until she hears some squeaking and can see it breathe. She then has to turn around and repeat this process until all the puppies are out. After repairing the uterus and sewing up the incisions, we tend to give the puppies a check over, looking for cleft palates and other developmental abnormalities.

When the bitch is safely awake again and the pups are happily breathing and squeaking for mum's milk, we can send them back home with the owner. Despite what seems a pretty big task for the veterinary team, the majority of us do enjoy performing caesarians or helping with the babies. Bringing life into the world is a wonderful thing to be able to do, so long as everything goes according to plan.

Obviously, there are several situations that can complicate things, starting with those calls that occur at night. In the middle of the night when you can't call in another member of staff to help you, the nurse who is 'on call 'with you has a very interesting juggling act ahead of them; they have to keep the bitch under a stable anaesthetic whilst also reviving puppies. If the anaesthetic becomes unstable at the same time, we always have to prioritise mum over the puppies and we then have to bring the owners in to help us revive the puppies. This can be difficult in itself if the owners are squeamish! Sadly, due to cost concerns or lack of knowledge, some people will leave their cat or dog pushing for far longer than they should do. It is a fairly terrible thing to have to perform a C-section knowing that some or even all of the puppies or kittens are dead. Given we can often find this out on ultrasound scan and it is not an emergency if the foetuses aren't alive, we will try several doses of oxytocin before resorting to putting the mum through such major surgery. If there is a chance than any of the babies are still alive, we will still rush to a caesarian and time is of the essence. If you ever see dark green discharge appearing from a whelping bitch or queen, it means that a placenta has separated from the uterus and the baby should appear very shortly. If not, bring them down to the vets. Often, the vibration of the car journey can stimulate more contractions and we occasionally find that they have whelped on the way down.

The mum is not out of danger either and I have known of a few dogs or cats that have died as a result of whelping or having a C-section. This is why we do not encourage breeding to be taken lightly! Even after giving birth naturally or via surgical intervention, we always tell owners to expect to lose at least one of the litter as nature is cruel and it is survival of the fittest. Some animals don't seem to realise that their puppies or kittens are their own, especially after a caesarian as they didn't go through the act of giving birth. We have had a cat just stand up and walk away from her kittens, never once feeding them and leaving them to the owners to bottle feed every two hours for the first two weeks. I have seen one French bulldog turn around, bite and kill some of her puppies. One of my colleagues once had a Bernese mountain dog brought in who had whelped naturally but the owners couldn't find the puppies anywhere. Only after x-raying the bitch did they realise that they were actually now in her stomach as she had eaten them.

Obviously, this is the minority but breeders need to be aware of the potential for heartbreak and danger for all involved. We are seeing increasing numbers of C-sections now because of the amount of dogs being bred. Although we like the act of performing the surgery and having a hand in bringing new life into the world, we don't particularly enjoy the amount of unhealthy bulldogs being bred. No bitch or queen should have more than two C-sections or three natural litters as it is a lot to put them through and considered unethical to overbreed them. When caesarians are needed just due to bad luck, as tends to happen in most cats or other dog breeds, it is often a very rewarding surgery to perform and the veterinary staff love getting involved with the babies. Those first loud squeaks reverberating through the walls of the practice is something we all love to hear.

PETS THAT ARE RESCUED FROM THE UK

We see quite a lot of rescue animals in our daily work as vets. They can be very rewarding pets for owners to have and giving some of these poor animals a home is a lovely thing to do. Due to a variety of reasons, thousands of pets end up in rescue homes each year. Sometimes this is because owners have passed away or moved into houses that don't allow pets, sometimes they are part of the stray population that have been caught and tamed, occasionally they are seized from poor homes but a lot of the time, they are there because people decide they don't want them or can't afford to pay for them anymore. Obviously, we would always encourage people to take them into rescue centres rather than just tossing them out on the street or drowning a bag of unwanted kittens, but if people could be more responsible and really think through getting a pet then this would be preferable. Luckily, there are a steady stream of people who want to rescue a pet rather than buying one as a youngster.

There are various advantages to getting a rescue pet. Some of them come well trained so you don't have to do all of this yourself. Getting older pets means you don't have to go through toilet training and the excitable puppy or kitten stage where they bite everything! You often already know the personality of the pet so if you want an older, calmer dog or a younger, energetic cat that's also good with other cats, then you can find one. A lot of the older generation of people will end up rescuing small dogs that are middle-aged or older that are much easier to handle. Young families may want a young cat that has shown to be good with children. They also tend to come with routine healthcare provided such as vaccinations, parasite treatment and neutering. This saves you the money on these things and also gives you some assurance that you are taking on a reasonably healthy animal.

Rescue centres will likely have had the pet in for a number of weeks to months so any obvious health conditions will have become apparent and either treated or discussed with the new owner, rather than being a surprise as the pet grows up. Good examples of this are things like allergic skin disease, hip and elbow dysplasia and cat flu. Older dogs may have arthritis and heart disease but this will already have been investigated and appropriate treatment started. Knowing from the outset that you are going to have to continue giving certain tablets, eye drops or stick to reduced exercise regimes means that you can have pets that fit into your lifestyle. Although long term medication can be costly, the initial payment for the investigation tends to be the more expensive part and this will have been done already by any good rescue centre. Some of the charities have schemes whereby they will pay for any ongoing medication for conditions that the pet has when you adopt it, which can be wonderful given insurance companies won't pay for pre-existing conditions.

The best thing about getting a rescue pet is the fact that you are really changing their lives for the better. A lot of them have been in the homes for weeks to months and even years. Suddenly having their freedom and a loving owner must be fantastic for them. You can really see how happy a lot of them are and what a bond they have with their new family. Some of the dogs can be wary at first, especially if they have come from a tricky background. Seeing them come out of their shell over the next few visits to the vets can be lovely to see.

There are the a few disadvantages of course. It can be a lot of work to make a feral cat into one that likes people. Some of them spend the first few days in their new homes hiding under the bed and can urinate all over the house due to stress. If they have come from distressing environments then their instinctive reaction is to swipe or hiss which can take time for a rescue home to change so they end up being in a kennel for quite a long time. Dogs can be even more difficult to get to a happy mental state. Seeing some of the dogs that have been mistreated can make you wonder how they could ever learn to trust a human again. This can make them anxious at best and fear aggressive at their worst. This behaviour can also be similar towards other dogs which is both a problem within the rescue homes and when the new owners want to take them out for walks. There are some dogs that we cannot examine because they freak out too much and some are so aggressive out of fear that we can't even get a muzzle on them. This is understandable at first and we can see why rescue centres try their best to train them to understand that humans can be kind and lead to good things. However, there have been quite a few situations now where, after months or even years of attempted socialisation, a dog or a cat is still very aggressive. This is not the animal's fault and it is very sad, but it does mean they are not rehomable. Some charities have dedicated units that are meant to house these pets for the rest of their lives, with no other contact with humans or animals because it is too stressful for the individual. A lot of vet staff, myself included, think that a 'no euthanasia policy' in this situation isn't always the right thing. Living their whole life in confinement is not a fair way to be; they are merely existing rather than living and it can be kinder for them to not be here anymore.

Recently, there has been an influx of pets coming from countries in Europe. Some of these are puppies bought and imported for individual owners. We have had Siberian husky puppies brought in from Russia because the soon-to-be owners wanted 'the real thing'. This poor puppy had come on a three day journey in a van with a load of other puppies and 24 hours after arrival, was in our hospital being treated for parvovirus. Even if he had had his vaccinations as the breeder said (his paperwork showed they weren't given at the correct times), being with many other dogs in crates all defaecating on each other and sharing germs, means his little immune system didn't stand too much of a chance. Luckily, after three days he went home and has made a full recovery since. There are also many imports of puppies from Europe and America that are to be used for breeding that come in with cropped ears which is barbaric and illegal in the UK. As well as these puppies, there are also the massive amounts of rescue dogs brought in by charities. These charities rescue stray dogs from various countries across Europe. Though maybe an unpopular opinion amongst said charities, most British vets would discourage this. This is due to the diseases that are present in Europe that are not in the British pet population. There are species of tick and worm that can be brought in on the dogs, with some tick-borne diseases much more prevalent on the continent than they are here, such as *Ehrlichia* and *Babesia* that cause a severe anaemia.

There is a disease called Leishmaniasis caused by a parasite transferred by sandflies in both cats and, more commonly, dogs. These sandflies are seen in the warmer climates in southern Europe and we have seen multiple cases brought in by dogs from Greece and Cyprus. The disease is difficult to test for and treat, with dogs often on lifelong medication. Sadly, the organisms can hide in the bone marrow for years and come out again at any time so even though they test 'negative', they sometimes aren't. They cause a variety of signs but the most devastating is kidney failure. We have now had to PTS three dogs at a young age due to this condition, others only getting better after days of hospital-isation. Luckily, given we don't have sandflies, the disease can-not be passed to dogs that don't travel but there is a worry that with climate change the flies will move further north. Plus, it is still devastating for the individual dogs and their families.

Worryingly, we are seeing cases of Brucellosis coming in from the Eastern European dog population, after previously being eradicated from the UK. This causes infertility and abortion in dogs but also lethargy and lameness. All of these diseases can be transmitted to humans too so can you see why we are wor-ried? There have even been several cases of Distemper in rescue dogs from Romania this year, meaning our vaccination for this is far from obsolete now. On top of this, given a lot of the stray dogs and cats have lived life on the streets and can sometimes be mistreated by humans, they are often terrified of other dogs and people too. A lot of the pets that are older than about 6-8 months when imported require months to years of socialisation and training. Some of them are never truly happy dogs and cats and don't understand confinement of any kind.

We can see why people resort to getting pets from abroad though, given the UK charities have such stringent criteria that families have to meet. If you want to rehome a dog, some of the charities require a 6ft fence around your garden, people to not be working out of the home for more than four hours at a time and for your house to be laid out in a certain way. Some of these measures are completely ridiculous. How about asking people if they intend to get a dog walker or take the dog to day care if they are sociable enough? Or making sure the garden is secure enough without the need for such a high fence? What is bizarre is that they will rehome to someone who is home all day and yet has no money to pay for health care. Even very experienced dog owners who have had multiple dogs throughout their time in their house who have all been cared for well, will be rejected be-cause their garden doesn't meet the criteria. My friend who is a vet was declined a cat because she worked all day! Who better to rehome to than a vet?! Cats go out for most of their day anyway! It is something that really does need to be changed to encourage people to rehome from UK centres instead of resorting to those from abroad. Yes, we all want to save the mistreated animals from every single place in the world and we don't want anyone to suffer but there are thousands of pets within our own country that need our help first.

FINDING THE RIGHT JOB

I am a very lucky vet who has found a job that I love and it happened to be my first ever job. I was there for six and a half years and only left in order to have the flexibility to travel around the world with my partner (terrible COVID timing, huh?) I fully intend on returning to that job in the future and my months of being a locum have so far confirmed in my mind that my first practice is the best practice for me. I am fortunate enough to be back at the practice as a locum for the summer whilst they are waiting for other vets to start. Some of my friends have not been so lucky and they have changed jobs many times in their careers. A lot of them have now managed to find the right job for them but some of them are still unsure.

Firstly, changing veterinary jobs for both vets and nurses can be due to simple reasons such as wanting to change from doing mixed animal practice to just small animals. Sometimes, people need to just find a practice that is closer to home. For nurses, it could be that there is already an established 'head' and 'deputy head' nurse and they want some career progression or that they simply don't want to continue in the practice that they trained at and be seen as the bottom of the nurse hierarchy. However, a lot of the time it can be due to the fact that the particular practice doesn't suit how you want to work; some are too quiet and people get bored (becoming much rarer in recent times!), some are too busy and you don't have time to work up cases properly; some have 'on call 'duties and long weekend hours which is better for clients but worse for staff, some do not and this is much less stressful but can lead to suboptimal care for clients or owners; some have longer hours and a day off, others have shorter working days but more days worked.

Then you have the problems with the individual practices themselves. From my own experiences and from those of my friends and former colleagues, these specific problem practices do seem to be few and far between. Having said that, there does seem to be a bit of a divide between independent practices and corporate practices. The best comparison is that between a small boutique shop on the high street and that of a large chain.

When you work in an independent practice, you often feel much more valued than in corporate companies. This makes sense really given corporates own many vet practices and you are just a number on a sheet of paper to the boss at the very top. Your immediate boss may care and may want to help you but they are often stopped at the next level up. Certainly, one of my very talented friends was recently at breaking point at her practice; each vet working flat out and complaining about the rota that was in place for each of them. Management decided to give them a new rota that 'would help them out'. Because said rota was made by some person in an office that was not a vet and had never actually stepped foot in the practice, that rota was even worse than the current one. After more complaints from the vets, nothing changed. Her immediate boss was asked by management only four days before her leaving date whether there was anything they could do to keep her (a vet's notice period tends to be about three months so they had had a lot of time to realise she was leaving and do something about it). Needless to say, three vets left that practice in the space of two months. In direct comparison, when my old independent practice was working flat out with staff shortages during the pandemic, we went down to only emergency treatments to relieve pressure from the routine consultations; we were given blocks in our consults to catch up and take a breath and the bosses came down from their office time to cover anything they could. One of my colleagues decided that she couldn't cope with the amount of 'on call 'shifts that we had to deal with, due a variety of reasons. One of the part-time vets wanted to increase her hours and just like that, the problem was solved. Due to how busy the practice is, we often have to do all of our phone calls and paperwork in any gaps between consults or ops. This was starting to drain the vets and now each vet has dedicated paperwork time each week where consults are not allowed to be booked.

Corporate companies tend to have targets they want staff to meet or certain actions they have to perform to maximise profits. What is important here is that it is not the individual vets, nurses and reception staff that want to make the money and a lot of them will ignore these suggestions. It is the middle management that are taking orders from the people up higher. One of the corporate companies tried to get me to do the 'walk of gain 'where I was to walk the client to the reception desk after every consult to hand them over to a receptionist, stating who they were and what medication they needed and when their next appointment should be. This was to stop people walking out without paying and to make sure they always booked a follow-up appointment, even if that was their vaccination in six months 'time. This is a locum position that I will not be going back to, and permanently struggles to recruit vets!

One of my friends is a 'head vet 'in another practice and is completely the opposite. He is told that he would get a bonus if he and all his team met their sales targets each year. He refuses to do this and happily lets the bonus slip away as he doesn't want to make money from people when it is not needed. Thus, although it is only the corporates that ever set these targets, it is in part to do with the people within that particular branch.

A friend that worked in a particularly busy London corporate said that she felt like they didn't care about the welfare of the staff so long as more money could be made from the situation. They would add consults onto the end of the day to mean she always left late; they would book the operations list so full that it was impossible to complete them all in the normal working day so she would work through her lunch break; they would book consult blocks that were 4-5 hours long with no break even to go to the toilet. At no point did she get a 'thank you' for all the extra work either. Obviously, she has now changed jobs and is much happier (at an independent practice). The other independent practice that I have locumed at only has four hours of consults spread across the whole day. Even if there were a couple of walk in appointments and emergencies, you knew that there was only a small amount of time that you'd be under pressure for. You'd have five hours in the middle of the day to perform operations, do paperwork and have a lunch break and they always had a cap on the number of operations, set according to the estimated length of time it would take each procedure.

It is worth pointing out that there are also advantages to working at corporate practices. Most of the independent practices are the ones still doing their own 'on call 'shifts, meaning increased hours and impact on mental health. Corporates tend to get night vets or hand over to specific providers that mean their day staff don't have to do the shifts. You may get lucky and work for one of the corporate companies that pays more than the minimum legal requirement for maternity or sick pay. They often have a strong HR department, meaning that if you do have any issues between staff members or in your personal life, there is a dedicated team to help you. At independent practices, the HR department tends to be someone else within the practice so can make things a bit more tricky. For example, one of my best friends was working at an independent practice where it was the boss that she had the issues with; he was a manipulative man who used to speak to her and other staff members in a derogatory and demanding way. She tried various things but eventually ended up leaving and is actually now much happier in a corporate practice.

There does also seem to be more regulation on vets or nurses working in corporate practices. Certainly, all the stories I've heard of vet staff providing suboptimal care to pets all come from very small independent places where they can get away with their behaviour. There is the independent practice I have previously mentioned where my friend wanted to report a vet to the governing body but was told she could be prosecuted for slander by said vet if things didn't go the right way.

For the pets and clients too, there can be advantages to the corporates. The pet health clubs that give you all the routine pet care are fantastic value and flexible with which parasite treatments can be used. A quick scale and polish is amazingly cheap and they must be making a loss on this; they just make up for it for the costs of removing teeth. It is the non-routine care that also escalates very quickly; some of the prices of ultrasounds and blood tests have been 50% higher at the corporates to make up for how cheap the routine care is. Again, this is not a blanket rule and I know some of my friends working in corporates where prices are actually cheaper than the nearby independent practice. Some of them working in the same corporations as the one where I was made to do the 'walk of gain' said they are not asked to do it. Others have worked in an independent practice where they were asked to admit things for tests rather than just trialling treatment as it makes more money.

I have seen or heard about practices that have recently been bought out by the corporates and it seems that it requires the staff within them to fight back against any bad changes that they are trying to make. One of my friend's says that their vets just refuse to do some of the suggestions but I wonder how many vets and nurses know that they can actually stand up to their new bosses? In this current climate, vets and nurses are in very short supply and every practice seems to be understaffed so there is no way that they can afford for you to hand in your notice or force you to leave. Therefore, stand your ground and refuse to accept anything that you think detriments yourself or your clients in any way. This can turn a practice that isn't quite right into one that you love and is indeed the right one for you.

What I love most about the majority of independent practices is that everyone is like a family and this is how I know that I have found the right job for me. You all rope in together to help the whole team as you know that if one part of the cog doesn't work, the wheel stops turning. If the phones are ringing non-stop and a vet walks past with a gap in consults, they will pick up the phone. If the nurses are short staffed because of illness or holiday, a vet will act as a nurse and hold animals or set up anaesthetics (though we are far worse at this than the nurses). Receptionists will also try to help as much as possible even if they are risking getting bitten. I've seen my bosses with mops and vacuums at the end of the day, doing the cleaning so the nurses can leave on time too. If the vets are manic, the reception team will only book in urgent things or make some of the appointments take up two gaps rather than one. The nurses will triage the emergencies and deal with whatever they can.

We all care about the animals, clients and even the business itself. We know that all the bosses have worked hard to get to where they are and we want the practice to function as well as possible for them as well as for the pets. Yes, our salaries are dependent on the business too but it is more than that. It's like when someone is house proud and makes everything the best it can be for guests; you have a sense of pride in the practice because you have all made it what it is and you want it to be everything it can be. When there are any arguments between staff or you don't agree with a new policy from the bosses, you take it personally and you care because it's like your family member has told you off or made this new decision without you and it hurts. Our bosses are like a weird cross between a parent and an older sibling and you want to make them proud of you and at the same time you want to slap them when they do something you don't agree with and cry at them when they suggest that you could have handled a situation in a different way.

The bosses reward our loyalty with fun days out for the staff, bunches of flowers or bottles of wine and even the odd bonus in our pay package if we have had a particularly busy time. There is always a terribly cringey speech made at each practice outing and none of the bosses are great at public speaking but they all want us to know that they appreciate the busy little family that we are. You know you've found the right job when you care about the practice as a whole and not just your individual merits as a vet or nurse.

When I left my first practice, I cried all day and felt like someone had taken a part of me away. All of my colleagues cried too, including my bosses and the practice manager. I pop in to see them all whenever I am back in the area. When I was back as a locum for the summer, even though it was busy and I had to do some 'on call 'shifts, I felt like I'd come home.

A PET THAT HAS ALL ITS WELFARE NEEDS MET

There is a difference between a pet that is really well looked after and one that just has its welfare needs met. In an ideal world, we would love for all pets to be well looked after and live their best life and this is something that a large portion of pets in the UK do get. To have every pet live like this is an unattainable and unrealistic target so all we really want is for the pet to have its welfare needs met, and by this I mean that 'the five freedoms 'are met. These were set out in 1965 by the government to improve animal welfare across the board, from livestock to pets. They are the rules that the RSPCA will use when trying to prosecute owners and we as vets have the final say on whether a pet's five freedoms are met:

Freedom from hunger and thirst

Freedom from discomfort

Freedom to express normal behaviour

Freedom from fear and distress

Freedom from pain, injury and disease

Sounds simple doesn't it? Hmm. Read on.

Freedom from hunger and thirst

Well, this seems like the most basic need for a pet and although it is still too much to ask for some morons of this world, 99.9% of the time this need is met. Any pet food in the UK has to meet certain specifications and all of them are safe and contain all the nutrients needed. There are some brands that we would prefer over others but even the cheapest foods will still be enough to give your pet reasonable nutrition. Freedom from thirst seems particularly easy to cater for, though just so you know, any pet over eight weeks only needs access to *water*, not any other liquids such as goats 'milk. Getting the right requirements for your small furries or exotic pets can be a bit trickier and the majority of health issues we see in reptiles will come down to dietary deficiencies or lack of the right light or heat source.

We do get seized pets brought into us by the RSCPA or the council that have not been looked after properly and some of these are underweight. This is very upsetting to see and we really feel for these creatures. However, these poor animals only make up a very small percentage of the population compared to those that are abused in entirely the opposite way. These are the pets that are morbidly obese. It brings vets joy to see slim pets as I would say they are starting to be the minority now. To not have to say 'he could do with losing a kilo or two 'and to exclaim that they are a lovely weight really makes us happy! I'm not about to claim that making your pet overweight counts as abuse but making them obese *does* as it makes them prone to a whole host of health issues. A fat dog will, on average, die two years earlier than a slim one so you are *literally* killing them with kindness. Fat cats and dogs will get arthritis and be in pain with their joints much earlier than slim ones. They are more likely to get a painful disease called pancreatitis and the large majority of diabetic animals we diagnose were overweight before the diabetes took hold. I once told an owner that their dog was fat and that it was likely to have been the reason we had just diagnosed them with diabetes. He remarked that he likes him being fat because 'it makes him happy'. Yes, well it also gives him diabetes which means he now has to suffer injections twice daily for the rest of his life and possibly go blind from diabetic cataracts.

Studies have been done on dogs, measuring their stress hormone levels when they are overweight and then again once they have reached a normal weight. The levels of the stress hormone are much lower in the slim animals. You may think that giving your pet excess food makes them happy and it does for those couple of minutes it takes to eat, but long-term it will make them more unhappy.

Cats are very difficult to diet because you can't force them to go for walks and if they go to eat the other cat's food or go into other homes, you can't control their calorie intake. However, there are ways around a lot of these problems such as microchip triggered food bowls, 'do not feed me 'collars, toys to encourage play and gentle discussions with your neighbours who like to give them treats. Neutered pets require about two thirds of the calories they had before they were neutered. Most pet owners are not aware of this and are too worried about their pet coming home after an anaesthetic to listen to our post-op speech, so this is one of the biggest reasons we see for overweight pets. 'Overweight' pets we can cope with but those that go into the 'obese 'category can actually be prosecuted by the RSPCA now. We have some dogs that come into see us that can barely walk because they are so fat. We know this is not due to a lack of love like those that are too thin, but it is due to too much love. It doesn't stop the fact that you are abusing them and we are completely behind the RSCPA for prosecuting owners for this.

Freedom from discomfort

This is actually referring to appropriate shelter and environment, something that is most relevant in farm animals. There are regulations as to what size pen each animal should have and the level of cleanliness that needs to be maintained. These regulations are better in the UK compared to a lot of countries but they could always be better. Most cats and dogs will have access to appropriate shelter and clean living, either within the home or on the farm or kennels. A shelter needs to protect them from the rain, excess sun and wind. Animals really don't need anything fancy - shown by the fact that your cat will choose to lie on a plastic bag rather than the lovely new cat bed you bought for them. For some people, this still seems beyond them and they choose to tie a dog up in a back garden with no shelter. I always wonder what the point of having a dog is in this situation, except to possibly bark at intruders. Well, an alarm system probably costs less money to feed and doesn't have any welfare needs so try that instead.

As previously mentioned, it is the more exotic pets that don't seem to have their welfare needs met in this situation. Rabbits need to be able to stand up on their back legs in their cage and the bigger, the better. The minimum living space is 1.1 square metres per rabbit, with an exercise space of three square metres. For reptiles, each species tends to need a different requirement for heat, light and humidity sources so please research properly before getting these pets. You may not think it but the wrong amounts of these elements can lead to diseases that are incredibly painful for the animal. We once had a tortoise brought in that was squishy rather than having a solid shell due to a calcium and vitamin D deficiency. The poor thing would squeak with pain every time it was picked up as the shell pushed against its organs. It is unethical not to provide the correct environment and we have all manner of exotic pets that have been seized by the RSCPA brought into us for inspection and owners can be prosecuted.

Freedom from fear and distress

This is the one that hurts the most and the one that most people will think of when talking about animal abuse. Yes, a lot of time that abuse is causing pain too but when that pain subsides, the animals are left with mental scars that are with them for life. Rescue centres are full of dogs that cower when a person raises a hand or holds a stick, remembering a time when they were hit. When people take on rescue dogs that have been seized from bad homes, they often have to teach them what love from a human is. All they've ever known from humans is fear and pain and this above anything makes me want to cry. There are some people in this world who think that animals are beneath them and don't deserve any kind of respect. These are the people who will hit an animal with a car and not stop to check it is ok or take it to a vet. They are the people who will poison animals on purpose. They are the people who steal dogs from loving homes to sell or use in fighting. They are the people who will crop dog's ears just because it is what the breed traditionally looks like, even though it inflicts pain. They are the people who will shoot cats with air guns, breaking their legs or embedding them in body cavities which I have seen happen three times in my career already. They are the people who get angry and take it out on their pet, causing fractures and bruises. The poor animal doesn't understand why this is happening to them when often they haven't even done anything wrong. They live their lives in fear of when it will happen again and sadly, over time, some of them react with fear aggression. These horrible people want to exert their dominance, power and control by bringing about fear and inflicting pain.

Stop reading this paragraph if you don't want to hear the worst of the abuse I've seen; I don't blame you at all for wanting to skip over it. One of my colleagues had to watch video footage from the RSCPA of a man tying a cat into a plastic bag, repeatedly kicking it and then urinating all over it. Recently, I saw what I hope will be the worst thing I will see in my career; a well-loved cat brought in by the police who had found it with its ears and tail cut off and half of its body skinned. Evidence suggested it was still alive when this occurred. My boyfriend will testify as to how much this affected me that evening after work, to think about the poor cat in its final moment, scared and in horrendous pain, not knowing why. I can't see how a cat would allow just one person to do this as it should have been able to get away so there must have been another person holding it down. I can only hope that I am wrong and the cat was drugged first to make it unconscious. It is not the first time this has happened - people consistently mutilate animals around the country and the world. The police are interested in these cases due to the fact that a lot of murderers and rapists start off by torturing animals. I hope that every person who purposely harms an animal out of malice gets their comeuppance one day and whatever they did to the animal gets done back to them. Our justice system is better than a lot of countries but animal abuse still doesn't get the sentencing it deserves.

There is also the unintentional distress and fear that owners inflict upon their pets without any sense of malice. Instead, it is again borne out of too much love. These are the pets, usually dogs, that are affected by separation anxiety. As vets, we love to see dogs that bound into the consult room or at least don't hide behind their owner's legs like a toddler being dropped off at nursery for the first time. As discussed previously, it is much better to leave your dog alone occasionally so it gets used to being left on its own. Even if you are at home most of the time in life, you take your dog with you everywhere and never leave it alone to go out for dinner with friends, you cannot assume that you are never going to need to leave it in exceptional circumstances. This includes if the dog becomes poorly and needs to be in with us for 24-48 hours. We sometimes have to give dogs sedative drugs because they are so distressed about being apart from their owners.

Sadly, occasionally owners have gone into hospital or passed away and the dog is left behind, taking months of behavioural therapy with family members or new owners before they are happy again. Please do leave your pets alone for a few hours a couple of times a week at a minimum, it will make their lives a lot easier in the long run. It also helps to expose them to cars, loud noises and other animals so that they don't get scared every time they hear a bang or another dog comes up to them in the park. Unfortunately, some dogs are naturally just more timid than others and will always have behavioural issues but trying to socialise them will make them that little bit less anxious.

Freedom to exhibit normal behaviours

The majority of the time, this refers to zoos and farm animals where they need to be able to be kept stimulated and enjoy their lives as much as they can. In pet animals, this need can be met by interaction with other animals or the best mimic you can provide. Cats that live indoors should be able to exhibit hunting behaviour by grabbing hold of toys that you dart around the floor. Dogs usually live in packs so they should be able to play with other dogs from time to time, or at least have play time with the owner. Some breeds like to sniff things on the ground, following scents and exhibiting tracking behaviour. Others are extremely intelligent and require constant stimulation or large amounts of exercise. Rabbits and guinea pigs are best housed with others to mimic colonies in the wild. Birds should be allowed out of a cage to fly in the house or have wings clipped so that they can still flap their wings and fly to a small extent outside but cannot fly away.

There is one main situation that occurs regularly that does not meet this welfare regulation for the animals. Dogs that are never walked or allowed to interact with others do not get to exhibit or mimic their normal behaviours and this is cruel. There have been many times that we hear of a dog that is only ever kept in a small yard or garden, regardless of whether it still gets shelter, food and water. Sometimes, they are just kept in an indoor pen or cage in the house. Some families use them as guard dogs, some just seem to think it is acceptable for them to never be taken out and of course, some are used as breeding machines.

There is a big difference between a commercial breeder who has multiple bitches but still keeps up with all the healthcare and welfare needs, and those that are 'puppy farms'. Commercial breeders will usually let all the bitches out for walks or runs in a paddock every day as well as giving them enough food, water and bedding in their pens. They're not living their best life and they don't get any home comforts but they have no welfare concerns. Most of them will have a few litters and then be re-homed when they are six or seven years old. 'Puppy farms 'do not give the bitches any semblance of a life. They are kept in pens, have their puppies and are put back into pup as soon as possible after the puppies have been homed. They don't get walked or get to play with other dogs thus tend to be quite fearful of human contact and other animals. They are bred for as long as they produce viable puppies and these puppies are never vaccinated or wormed, often coming into us with their new owners for their first vaccines riddled with fleas, mites and worms, underweight or with diarrhoea. It is very difficult to tell the difference between these two set of breeders on first glance but having some paperwork for the pup is always a good start. Cats can be bred in an equally terrible way and not get to experience the life that an animal should have. Sadly, people just think they can make money off animals and if things don't go the right way, they just leave the animal to die in pain or toss it out onto the street.

A lot of people tell me that they think that a cat or dog being able to have babies is part of what a life should hold and that they want their pet to experience it. I guess you could say that allowing them to have a litter is 'exhibiting normal behaviour'. Personally, I don't think that animals have the same mothering desires that we do and they wouldn't know or care if they didn't have a litter. The fact that I have seen some cats just stand up and walk away from their newborn kittens, or seen a dog who has turned around and eaten her new pups, rather shows that this is the case. However, if you do believe this then we will always support your decision to do so as long as it is done properly. With dogs, bitches should be at least two years old, preferably three before they have a litter. If she has any medical conditions that can be genetic, or any behavioural traits that are undesirable then she shouldn't be bred from. The sire should be picked with the same care. The mum should be vaccinated so she passes this immunity to the puppies and they are protected until the maternal antibodies wane at 10-12 weeks old and they get their own vaccines. She should be up to date with flea and worming treatment and the puppies then wormed too. Owners should be prepared for everything to go wrong and be able to put in the time hand rearing puppies if the mum rejects the litter, the expense of vet visits and C-sections if needed and the emotional side that comes with losing any of the pups or even the mum herself. So long as owners aren't just going into breeding to make some money, then breeding can be a lovely and natural thing for a dog and the family.

The same can be said for cat breeding but the issue with them is that you cannot control when they get pregnant if they are let outside. Female cats, or 'queens', will become pregnant anytime from about five months old. This is the equivalent to a young teenage girl, who has just hit puberty, becoming pregnant. The body puts a lot of its energy requirements into growing the kittens and so the mother suffers because of it, stunting growth and development. A couple of weeks after the kittens are born, she can get pregnant again and thus the cycle continues. They can lose litters or the queen herself can die in labour as she is not strong enough, leaving owners with several kittens to feed every two hours. If you really want a litter, we strongly recommend that you keep your cats inside the house until they are old enough to be bred, at 18-24 months old. If you want to let them out sooner, please do get them neutered so you are not putting stress on your cat's young body. There are enough cats in rescue centres that need homes without adding the thousands of unwanted kittens that are born each year. This is especially true if the mother is unvaccinated and passes cat flu to all the kittens, meaning they have regular eye and respiratory infections all their lives. On top of all this, have you ever seen or heard cats mating? It is very violent and tends to involve the male holding down the female with his teeth on the back of her neck; his penis has barbs on it that point backwards when erect so it is painful for the female to pull away. Do you really want to put your queen through this, or allow your tom cat to do this to others?

Freedom from pain, injury and disease

Well, I think this is probably the 'freedom 'that isn't met most often. Vets love it when owners follow guidelines and do everything they can in life to prevent disease and pain. There are the top class owners who clean their pet's teeth, vaccinate them yearly, keep their nails short and their coat groomed, seek veterinary advice whenever needed and provide appropriate treatment. I am not saying that every pet has to have all of these done to have their welfare needs met but there are so many dogs and cats that we see that don't even meet one of these criteria. Sometimes, we have to shave an entire dog or cat because it is so matted. I don't think many people are aware of how painful having a matt of fur can be once it reaches the point where it is pulling on the skin, let alone the fact that it holds urine, faeces and mud so can cause skin infections. We regularly see cats who's nails have grown all the way around and back into their pads. This happens because they don't shed their nails as they get older and they are rubbish at showing you pain. We have some dogs that come in in similar states, looking like those dogs that you see on charity adverts in the 'before 'photos. This is fairly unacceptable and if your pet is grumpy enough not to let you or the groomer keep it in reasonable condition, you can join the many animals that come in to see us every 3-6 months to be sedated for grooming. If you start with nail clips and coat brushing from the start then you are more likely to be able to do it yourself ongoing. Animals that have light burdens of parasites such as fleas, ticks and worms are not welfare issues so long as they are treated when they start to cause any issues. Those that have clearly had fleas for months, where there is barely any hair left on their back and their skin is weeping from infection where the pet has been chewing - this is a welfare issue.

Neutering your pet can also be a very responsible way of preventing diseases, such as pyometra and mammary tumours in bitches as previously mentioned. For male dogs, the medical benefits of castration are not as great and it is for behavioural reasons that we castrate a lot of them, or we leave them entire. Obviously, if there are not testicles present then testicular tumours do not occur and they have fewer prostate issues but these issues can often be helped by castration at the time of presentation and is never an emergency situation. The only time you *need* to remove a testicle early is if one testicle is retained in the body - this will turn cancerous as the dog gets older so must be removed before this happens. The benefits of spaying female cats has been mentioned and we do also see pyometras in cats too. Males cats can impregnate females from 4-5 months of age and should also be neutered before being let outside. Entire males are more likely to roam for females thus get into more car accidents. They fight over territory more so get abscesses and can pass Feline Leukaemia Virus (FeLV) by biting, or sexually transmitted diseases such as FIV (the feline equivalent to HIV). Both these diseases increase risk of normal infections becoming life-threatening and of getting cancer. If you cannot afford to neuter your cat, then many cat charities will offer vouchers, so there is no excuse. Some people argue that neutering dogs actually makes them more prone to certain diseases such as urinary incontinence in females. There does seem to be an anecdotal link but no studies have ever been able to prove this. Incontinence can be helped with medication and is never life-threatening, unlike a pyometra or mammary cancer. Joint problems are more likely if larger dogs are neutered early so we advise waiting until they are over 12-18 months of age. Bone tumours in rottweilers have extensively been studied and they have found the lowest risk of getting these tumours comes from neutering between one and two years of age, not before and not if left entire. The most common issue we see after neutering is weight gain as the hormones use up a lot of energy, thus cutting the food by a third once neutered is the way to stop this. Certain breeds can get coat changes when neutered but this is purely cosmetic. I've never seen any personality changes except dogs becoming less bouncy and unruly which is probably no bad thing.

Vaccination is another battle we face regularly which is a whole other story but if you don't believe in vaccinations, please at least bring your pet to the vet every year or two for a general checkover as they get older. We can pick up on things early like heart problems, dental disease, lumps and arthritis. In non-painful conditions such as organ dysfunction, to not treat is not a welfare issue but if we do tell you your pet is in pain with it's joints, teeth, cancerous lumps, abdominal issues or whatever reason, you are not meeting the welfare needs of your pet if you don't give it pain relief. This is the minimum that we require and if you cannot afford this, or you don't agree with conventional pain relief, then please ask us what you can do to reduce costs or any alternative therapies that we can suggest. We are legally required to provide emergency pain relief for free so if your pet has been involved in an accident, please don't let costs put you off bringing them down as we can at least give them some strong pain relief whilst we discuss options.

Obviously, in an ideal world, no pet should forego treatment of any disease, regardless of whether it is painful or not. It is in this situation that insurance can be very helpful. Not many people can afford hundreds to thousands of pounds for vet bills without any warning. Thus, paying the insurance company £20-60 a month for insurance is much more manageable. Premiums can go higher than that for certain breeds such as French bulldogs but if you're going to spend several thousands of pounds on a 'designer' breed, my sympathy is limited if you didn't leave room in your finances for its ongoing care. Lifetime cover is the best as it means if your pet gets a lifelong condition such as diabetes, the cost of care is covered for life and not just the first year of the condition. This also stops insurance companies getting out of paying for conditions later on that a pet may have had previously in its life. For example, some companies will try to avoid paying for a bad case of vomiting when a dog is old and needed hospitalisation because it also vomited a few times as a puppy after eating something it shouldn't. Having cover of fees of at least £3000 is advised to cover anything that doesn't need a referral to a specialist. If you can only afford the cheaper policies of up to £1000 for one year, this at least means we can treat the majority of basic accidents or injuries, or the cost of painkillers and anti-itching drugs for the year.

Insurance does not cover routine treatment such as neutering, costing £60-120 for a cat, or £150-500 for a dog depending on the size and sex. They don't cover the costs of vaccinations, usually £40-60 a year, but require you to have them or at least a health check yearly. If you cannot afford the insurance costs, or neutering or vaccination costs, then you should consider whether you should have a pet. In some countries in the world, owners need to pass a test on pet care and a financial check before they are allowed to own a pet. As animals get older, if they have had many health issues in their life, their premiums can rise to a more unmanageable level. Often these premiums are still under the costs of medications if your pet has multiple health conditions. If they don't have any ongoing medication, it can be worthwhile to put aside the money that you would otherwise spend on insurance into a separate account so you have a buffer of money if something does go wrong. If it doesn't, you've not lost any money in the process and if your boiler or car breaks instead, you've got the money for that.

As a profession, we are fed up of people saying we care more about money than we do about the animals. I really hope the previous chapters go some way to dispelling this myth. However, we really can't go around giving out free or cost price treatments all the time, or have owners letting charities pay for everything and using up their funds. **Having a pet is not a right, it is a privilege.** We often get people shouting at us for 'letting their pet suffer'. We have taken an oath that means we will never let a pet suffer. If you call us in the middle of the night to your cat who has been hit by a car, we will see them for free if you cannot afford it, we will give them emergency pain relief whilst you contact friends and family for money, call charities for you and see what costs we can cut to give reasonable but not 'gold standard' care. At the end of all this, we will also offer euthanasia for free. It is much better to put an animal to sleep and stop it being in pain. We then get yelled at for 'killing 'the pet rather than saving it. Well, no, *you* are the one who is forcing us to make this horrible decision because we have no other option. We hate doing it and luckily it doesn't happen very often at all but it really sticks with you when it does. It is no secret that having a pet costs money and if you didn't prepare for that then this is entirely your fault and not ours. You can't just go to the supermarket and ask for free food, ask a plumber if he can fix your burst pipe for cost price of the parts, or refuse to get car insurance because you choose to spend your money on the latest mobile phone or packs of cigarettes instead. I once had an owner tell me she could't afford to pay the £70 for the consultation and treatment of her cat's painful abscess on its leg because 'that was her spending money for a holiday to Spain next week'. You are responsible for a living creature, get your priorities right. Yes, I know I am ranting (again) but do you know how hard it is not to be able to say this to people in real life?

What vets *do* like are owners that come in and ask our advice on what we they can do for the best and listen to our advice. I've had owners come in for their pet's yearly vaccination when they are older and just ask for a full blood test to check all their organ function even though they seem healthy! This is amazing care and something that even some of us vets and nurses don't do. Don't get me wrong, 80-90% of the animals we see will meet the welfare standards of 'the five freedoms', you just can't help but dwell on those that don't. We have some incredible clients who have chosen to forego new cars, remortgage their houses or give up other luxuries so they can pay for unexpected costs. We don't need quite this level of care though. We just love those people that hear us saying their pet needs to lose some weight and when we see them six months later, they are an ideal weight. We like people who put their pet on joint supplements because we tell them they are starting with arthritis. A couple of years later, when we tell them their pet now needs painkillers of some kind, we like those that use them. We like owners who are horrified when they are told their cat actually has fleas under the surface and happily pay for good flea treatment for the next three months. We like owners that book in for a dental procedure when we say their pet's teeth are causing them pain. When a pet is clearly suffering, with no hope of successful treatment, we like owners who choose to put them to sleep. We especially like people who choose to make this decision before the pet has been suffering for many days to weeks. We like people who choose to neuter their pets but we also like those that choose to breed responsibly. We like owners who socialise and expose their pet to enough to stop them becoming afraid of everything. We like pets that enjoy their life no matter whether it is a working dog that lives outside in a kennel, a posh cat who will only the high-end cat food or a snake that can roam around a large vivarium, basking under heat lamps.

THANK YOU FOR READING

So there we have it; a collection of stories and rantings that were very therapeutic for me to write and, hopefully, enjoyable or informative for you to read. For those within the veterinary profession, I hope you felt some solidarity in your difficult days, nodded along with the vet advice and had a laugh that some of these misfortunes weren't yours. To anyone wanting to become a vet, nurse or any other member of a veterinary team, please see that the amazing sides of the job do make it worth it but you have to be able to cope with the difficult times. To the pet owners and other animal lovers, I hope you found some chapters educational when it comes to pet care and about the emotional sides of our jobs. I hope that you giggled at all the funny things pets have done that have brought me joy. I couldn't imagine doing any other job and love that every day is different. We've always got a story to tell; one of my colleagues performed a C-section recently and there was a kitten with two heads! One of the reception staff reminded me of the trick we played on her when we gave her a bag of 'elastic bands' and asked if she could get one out for us. They weren't elastic bands; it was a bag of worms that had been inside a dog that an owner had washed and asked us to identify. She screamed when she put her hand inside and luckily forgave us. You don't get this level of closeness to so many of your colleagues and clients in other jobs; you certainly don't get to cuddle animals and you don't get to have such highs to balance the lows.

If you have any other stories to share, please send me a message or post on Facebook or @stuffvetslike on Instagram, I'd love to hear from any of you. I've chosen to remain anonymous so as to not have any backlash on my place of work or on myself personally. I welcome any comments; good, bad or ugly in this professional context.

References

References - https://www.vettimes.co.uk/news/spvs-2020-salary-survey-released/

https://www.nurses.co.uk/careers-hub/nursing-pay-guide/

https://www.nao.org.uk/wp-content/uploads/2017/01/NHS-Ambulance-Services.pdf

https://www.healthcareers.nhs.uk/explore-roles/doctors/pay-doctors

https://www.vettimes.co.uk/news/spvs-2020-salary-survey-released/